W9-CNN-783

TALES OF THE
HEAVENLY CITY

Special Excerpt Edition
Featuring Rabbi Yehoshua Leib Diskin

by
Menachem Gerlitz

CIS
P·U·B·L·I·S·H·E·R·S
New York · London · Jerusalem

Published and distributed
in the U.S., Canada and overseas by
C.I.S. Publishers and Distributors
180 Park Avenue, Lakewood, New Jersey 08701
(908) 905-3000 Fax: (908) 367-6666

Distributed in Israel by
C.I.S. International (Israel)
Rechov Mishkalov 18
Har Nof, Jerusalem
Tel: 02-518-935

Distributed in the U.K. and Europe by
C.I.S. International (U.K.)
89 Craven Park Road
London N15 6AH, England
Tel: 81-809-3723

Cover credits: Deenee Cohen
Typography: Devorah Rozsansky

ISBN 1-56062-133-8

PRINTED IN THE UNITED STATES OF AMERICA

TABLE OF
CONTENTS

A GAON
IN THEIR MIDST

The Afikoman Gift

Yerushalayim's Jews were thrilled to carry out the Brisker Rav's slightest hint of a wish. They treasured his every holy movement, exulted at the hope of a blessing from his holy lips. One who was fortunate enough to actually receive his benediction was considered a lucky man, for hadn't the Jews of Yerushalayim seen, with their own eyes, how the *tzaddik* decreed and G-d fulfilled?

Sara, the daughter of Rav Akiva Yosef Schlesinger, longed for such a blessing for her nine-year-old son. She constantly prodded her husband David to take their little Zalmanke in to Rav Yehoshua Leib Diskin for a *berachah* that the boy grow up to be a pious Jew. Each time, David would put her off.

"I can't do it," he argued. "One doesn't go in to the Brisker Rav just like that and ask for a *berachah*. It may seem a simple thing to a woman, but it just isn't done! Even great men hesitate

7

to enter his chamber and tremble in fear before his holy presence. What do you want from me, a mere young man?"

David went further and told his wife about the letter that the Brisker Rav had just received from one of the leaders of the generation, the renowned Rav Yosef Dov Ber Soloveichik, author of *Beis Haleivi* and present Rav of Brisk. This great person had written, "My hands have been trembling for two weeks since I began writing this letter to the great Rav Yehoshua Leib Diskin."

"And if our leaders approach the Brisker Rav with such trepidation, what should I say?" he concluded.

Sara heard all of his explanations and his hesitations but did not change her mind. On the contrary, the more he exalted the figure of the *rav*, the greater grew her desire to have her son blessed by him. Yet the harder she persisted, the firmer grew his refusal.

"I am too much awed by him," he would reply.

As the holiday of *Pesach* approached, Sara began to renew her request with fresh fervor. "You are among the top ten disciples of the *rav*," she argued. "You were chosen to found his *yeshivah*, Ohel Moshe. Is it so hard for you to enter and ask him to bless your child?"

David did not give in.

When this righteous woman saw that her tears did not move him, she devised a different plan. On *Erev Pesach*, she called her Zalmanke to her and coached him in his role. At the *seder* table, he was to snatch away the *afikoman*. Then, later, he was to refuse to return it until his father agreed to take him in to the *rav* for a blessing.

Zalman was both naive and cunning. His quick hands stole the coveted *afikoman* while his father was telling the epic of the redemption from Egypt. When the time came to eat the *afikoman*, David noticed that it was gone, according to custom. He had no idea, however, that this time he would have to pay dearly to redeem it.

"I'll buy you a copy of *Nefesh Hachaim*," he offered in exchange for the *matzah*.

Zalmanke was not to be bought off so easily.

"I'll buy you a *Pnei Yehoshua*," David suggested.

He refused. Prize after prize was dangled before him, but Zalmanke accepted none of his father's offers, wanting only what his mother maintained was rightfully his—a blessing from the Brisker Rav. Sara sat facing him across the *seder* table and smiled to Zalmanke, encouraging him not to give in until he extracted the promise from his father.

It was getting late, and David clearly saw that he had no choice but to give in to the boy. Unable to promise, he consented to try with all his might. Zalmanke, who could not expect more than that, relinquished the *afikoman* with a beaming face.

When the first day of *Chol Hamoed Pesach* arrived, Zalmanke reminded his father of the promise. There was no way out, and so, as soon as David returned from *Mussaf*, he announced to his happy household that he would finally take Zalmanke to the Brisker Rav. Sara's heart pounded with joy. Her lips murmured a prayer that this hour would be favorable, an opportune time for the *berachah* to flow without interference from the *tzaddik* to the boy.

David took the dancing little boy by his hand, and they went together toward the *rav's* house. The boy's face expressed boundless joy. Just a little while longer and the great Brisker Rav would place his saintly hands upon Zalmanke's head and bless him. Finally!

9

They reached the house and even approached the *rav's* study. David took a peek through a crack to see in what setting he would find the *rav*. His eyes took in the *rav's* holiday garb and the holy face that was illuminated with majesty. He was seated on his chair, deeply immersed in thought. The room was completely quiet. To his left and right were famous *rabbanim* of the city. Rav Yosef Chaim Sonnenfeld, Rav Hirsh Michel Shapiro, Rav Yeshaya Orenstein and his son Rav Yaakov, Rabbi Naftali Hertz Halevi of Jaffa and Rav Eliezer Dan Ralbag were all sitting in meditation and trepidation without moving a limb. All eyes were turned toward the central figure of the *rav* which glowed with holiness and whose spirit transcended their mortal surroundings.

David took this all in with a brief glance and shied back quickly. This was surely not the time to open the door and enter! His heart beat wildly and taking his son's hand, he stepped further back, prepared to go home empty-handed with the disappointed Zalmanke. But at this point, the boy burst into tears.

The *rebbetzin*, hearing the youthful weeping, hurried to see what caused it. She recognized the boy and offered him almonds and sweet wine to still his cries, but he continued sobbing bitterly.

"What do you want, Zalmanke?" she asked him with motherly concern. "Tell me, and I'll give it to you."

But Zalmanke, unable to speak because of his choking sobs, did not answer.

"Where is your father?" she asked him. When he pointed to the outer room, she went to ask David why the child was weeping so intensely.

"He wants a *berachah* from the *rav*," the father answered.

"Well, well," she replied good-naturedly, "if he has shed such a multitude of tears for it, he surely deserves one. I myself will take him inside to the *rav*."

Within seconds, they had entered the room. The *rav* had just shaken off his state of semi-trance and now listened to his wife's plea. He then raised his palms, placed them upon the small head of the boy and blessed him.

"Let it be G-d's Will that you be an '*ehrlicher Yid*,' a true Jew," the *rav* said.

The boy himself joined in the "*Amen*" that everyone heartily pronounced. And David, who had meanwhile gone to his son's side, managed to say that one word, too, before a torrent of tears gushed down his face.

Meanwhile, Sara stood expectantly by her window. Her eager eyes impatiently scoured the street for some sign of the returning heroes. Suddenly, she saw the flying figure of Zalmanke catapulting toward home. She ran out to catch her happy offspring in joyful arms with a prayer of thanks on her lips that G-d had fulfilled her request.

It is interesting to note that the very window upon whose sill she leaned and waited so eagerly, the window of Rav Akiva Yosef Schlesinger's home, faced the *Kosel Hamaaravi*. The single pane of glass had been bathed with numerous prayers and tears. Liba, the wife of Rav Akiva Yosef and daughter of Rav Hillel of Kolomya, used to stand at this very window and pour out her prayers to the One Who had caused His Name to dwell in the holy place that she could clearly see in the distance. Her prayers revolved around one theme—that the coming generations, fruit of her womb, would be righteous men, men of integrity, *tzaddikim*.

Rebbetzin Liba offered another *tefillah* on Thursdays from

the same window. She would pray that the objects of value that she still owned would fetch a good price at the pawnshop so that she would have the money needed to cover her *Shabbos* expenses. She begged G-d to invest her with grace in the eyes of the dealer so that he would give her the needed coin.

And they say that Liba's prayers were almost always answered.

"An *ehrlicher Yid*" was the *berachah* that the Brisker Rav bestowed upon little Zalmanke, son of Reb David, and that is what he became. From that momentous day until his death, Zalmanke was enveloped with an aura of holiness, abstinence and purity. All of his deeds were solely for G-d's sake.

One *Chol Hamoed Succos* found the entire city in a state of confusion bordering on hysteria. Rav Hirsh Michel Shapiro, one of the beloved Jews of the city, had suffered a serious fainting spell, some kind of stroke. The city reverberated with prayers for his quick recovery. When he awoke from his prolonged faint and regained consciousness, his family wished to remove him from the *succah* to the safety and comfort of his home. Although he resisted with his last ounce of strength, he was easily overpowered by his well-intentioned family who carried him into his house, in accordance with the *halachic* decision of the Brisker Rav.

When he was safely inside, the members of his family asked him why he had fought them so vigorously.

"I thought that was my last hour. I didn't want to willingly desert the dear *mitzvah* of *succah* at that crucial time," he explained.

Even within the confines of his home, however, Rav Hirsh Michel's condition was critical. The people of Yerushalayim ran to the *Kosel Hamaaravi* to pray for his speedy recovery;

12

others sped to the graves of *tzaddikim* on Har Hazeisim to beg them to intervene for him in Heavenly circles; still others went to inform the Brisker Rav and to join him in prayer.

In the midst of this confusion, it was discovered that fourteen-year-old Zalamanke had disappeared. Zalmanke's mother was the only one who was not worried. "He is surely hiding in some *shul* and saying *Tehillim* for Rav Hirsh Michel," she reassured her worried husband.

Day waned, and night swept over the city. Still no Zalmanke. Reb David suddenly thought of looking for Zalmanke's *lulav* and *esrog*. They were gone. Evidently Zalmanke had intended on staying wherever he was until the following morning. But where can the boy have gone? his father wondered.

All the night David worried, but the next morning Zalmanke appeared with another boy. He was carrying his *lulav* and *esrog* in his right hand, and in his left, a pair of shoes. The boy walked in barefoot.

"Where have you been, Zalmanke? And why are you barefoot?" his family rained questions upon the boy's head.

All the answers revolved around Reb Hirsh Michel's sudden fainting spell. As Zalmanke's travelling companion explained to the family, the boy had been present when the *tzaddik* took ill. All shaken up by it, he had run home to grab his *lulav* and *esrog* and had then gone to his friend. The friend had hired a donkey and they had set off for Chevron to *daven* at the graves of our forefathers at the Mearas Hamachpeilah.

The two boys had spent the entire night in *tefillah*, which they culminated with a dip in the *mikvah* of the kabbalist, Rav Eliyahu Mani, and with *vasikin* prayers. Then they had headed homeward.

When they were well on their way, the friend remarked that

Zalmanke's shoes looked strange. "You must have switched shoes with someone else at the *mikvah*," he told him.

Zalmanke quickly too, off the offending shoes. "It amounts to robbery," he said, "to wear someone else's shoes. Let us return to Chevron so that I can seek out the owner of the strange shoes."

But his friend refused. "It would take too much time to track down the owner. Besides, your parents are probably worried enough about you as it is."

Zalmanke was forced to agree but travelled the entire way back to Yerushalayim barefoot.

When David heard the story of the shoes, he grew angry. "You should have returned to Chevron right away to seek the owner of the shoes. You do not let a *mitzvah* slip out of your hands at an opportune moment."

And so, that very day, Zalmanke returned to Chevron to seek the owner of the shoes. It was not in vain that the people of Yerushalayim pointed to Zalmanke as a personification of the Brisker Rav's blessing. As for Zalmanke, the true Jew, his prayer may have been the one that gained another year of life for Rav Hirsh Michel.

A *Kesubah* Found

Tziporah, wife of the Yerushalayim zealot Rav Yeshaya Orenstein, was a commendable, righteous woman. From the day of her marriage, she had never disturbed her husband from his Torah studies for any household matter, for even the slightest moment. One bright day, however, she made her appearance at the Ohel Moshe *yeshivah* in the Old City to rouse her husband from his *Gemara*. What had happened?

Tziporah had just visited the offices of the Ohel Moshe *yeshivah* situated right by the home of Rav Yehoshua Leib Diskin to redeem her *Yizkor* pledge. When she emerged, the transaction completed, she noted a flurry of torn papers on the office steps. For some reason they attracted her attention and she picked them up. She was shocked to discover that they were torn remnants of a *kesubah*.

"Perhaps some woman lost her *kesubah*," she now explained to her husband. "Since the *halachah* specifies that a woman may not live with her husband without a *kesubah* and since I have no further knowledge in these affairs, I am telling you, Yeshaya, to concern yourself with this matter."

Rav Yeshaya studied the shreds of decorated paper and realized that his wife was right. Before him were the remnants of Reb Ben Zion Yadler's *kesubah*. The wedding had taken place just the night before in the courtyard of the Brisker Rav's house. How had the *kesubah* been lost so soon? Who had ripped it up? Not being of an inquisitive or speculative nature, Rav Yeshaya hurried to the *chasan's* father, Reb Yitzchak Zev, to report his find.

Rav Yeshaya entered the courtyard just as Reb Yitzchak Zev was coming out to greet him with reproach for not having participated in his son's wedding the previous evening. Rav Yeshaya apologized, excusing himself on the grounds of preoccupation with communal affairs.

"Nevertheless, you missed something special, my good friend," Reb Yitzchak Zev informed Rav Yeshaya. "Sit down for a while and let me tell you about the greatness and singlemindedness of your *rebbe*, the Gaon of risk."

Before Rav Yeshaya had a chance to explain the purpose of

his visit, Reb Yitzchak Zev had already launched into his own account. "The Rabbi of Brisk was asked to officiate at my son's wedding last night. Everything was all set; the *chuppah* poles stood in place; the *chazan* had finished singing the '*Mi Adir*' traditional greeting for the *chasan*; the candles had been lit and the *chasan* and *kallah* had already marched down towards the *chuppah*. The Brisker Rav was checking the *kesubah* form for the third time when he suddenly noticed two words which appeared at the edge of the paper, Lunz Press. The *kesubah* form had been printed at the press owned by Avraham Moshe Lunz, one of the first *maskilim* in Yerushalayim, known for his support of the secular school environment.

"These words inflamed the rabbi who tore up the *kesubah* instantaneously and waited until another one was fetched."

Rav Yeshaya's eyes lit up. He had learned the secret behind the torn segment of the *kesubah*. Wishing Reb Yitzchak Zev much *nachas* from his son, he left. But he did not dispose of the torn *kesubah* pieces. "These fragments," he said, "should be preserved as a testimony for the coming generations of the Brisker Rav's battle against secular schools and the *maskilim* who dared threaten the purity of our education."

From that time on, Rav Yeshaya would produce these paper shreds to demonstrate the greatness of the Gaon of Brisk to various guests visiting the Holy City.

Some two years after the Brisker Rav passed away, Rav Yeshaya was sent abroad on a fundraising mission on behalf of Yeshivas Ohel Moshe and the Diskin Orphanage. When he reached Karlin he was invited to stay with the local rabbi, Reb David'l Friedman. Reb David'l had always maintained close contact with the renewed settlement in Eretz Yisrael and had constantly supported and encouraged it. Now that one of the esteemed, nobler souls of the Yerushalayim community had come to visit, he was overjoyed. Reb David'l begged his visitor to give a first-hand account of the Holy City's spiritual and material situation. Rav Yeshaya began talking about life in Yerushalayim, going from one topic to another. His conversation touched on the great zeal shown by the Brisker Rav in his battle against secular schools and *Maskilim*, as witnessed by the torn *kesubah*.

Reb David'l listened to his account, skepticism evident upon his face, but Rav Yeshaya merely produced the torn pieces of paper which he happened to have along. Reb David'l was impressed and moved. He gave a deep sigh and said, "*Oy, oy,* how little we in the Diaspora know of the battle waged by the Gaon of Brisk."

The Rabbi of Karlin was so overwrought with emotion elicited by the story, that he begged his guest to repeat it again word for word that same evening in the presence of one of the communal heads and to lend it credence by again producing the bits of *kesubah* on the table.

That evening, after *maariv* prayers, Reb David'l sent for Reb Yona Lerner, the *parnass*. Reb Yona appeared without delay. The host served the two men seated at his table some tea and then signalled to Rav Yeshaya to begin his story. The latter duplicated the account, emphasizing certain points, elaborating on others. For added effect he then produced the paper bits, laying them on the table in full view. Reb Yona looked at them and a tear rolled down his cheek.

Rav Yeshaya did not realize the rabbi's motive in this invitation. By the morrow, however, it all became clear when he learned from the Karlin inhabitants that this Yona was one of the wealthiest men in the city, a communal figure of stature. For some time he had supported a well known *maskil* in his efforts to establish a progressive school in Karlin, and none of the rabbi's arguments had succeeded in diverting him. Upon hearing Rav Yeshaya's story, however, not only did Yona cease his support of the reformer, but he became the man's sworn enemy. To show his repentance Yona decided to establish in nearby Pinsk a *Talmud Torah* for pure Jewish education. Yona maintained this institution throughout his lifetime, paying teachers' salaries from his own private pocket.

When Rav Yeshaya returned to Eretz Yisrael and related this chapter of Yona in Karlin to the elderly *kabbalistic* Rabbi of Chevron, Rav Shimon Menashe, the latter commented, "How amazing are the deeds of the Gaon of Brisk, who with the ripping up of a *kesubah* in Yerushalayim many years ago was able to establish a *Talmud Torah* in distant Pinsk many, many years later!"

Seventy Years Later

Rabbi Eliyahu Meir Zuldon, who lived in a tiny house at the edge of the Meah Shearim *shchunah*, was so old that he verily creaked with age. His senses still functioned perfectly, despite the yoke of years, though his appearance belied the strength hidden in his frame. When he debarked at Jaffa port upon his emigration from Grodna, Lithuania in 5655, the Arab dockworkers gaped at him, amazed that such an elderly man should have had the courage and enterprise to leave his birthplace and alone settle in Yerushalayim.

Customs officials estimated his age at ninety-plus. The Turkish doctor who was posted by the outer gate and liberally handed out the henna herb, which was acclaimed in those days as being especially beneficial in preventing cholera, estimated him to be one hundred. Actually, they all missed the mark.

The elderly *Maggid* of Vilkamir, Rabbi Chaim Yitzchak Rappaport, who knew Rabbi Eliyahu Meir from Russia, asserted that Rabbi Eliyahu had most certainly passed the hundred mark some while back. And his opinion, the people of Yerushalayim knew, was one which could certainly be relied upon.

The *Maggid* lavishly praised Rabbi Eliyahu's broad Torah knowledge, in particular his phenomenal memory. Rabbi Eliyahu, he insisted, was like the proverbial lime pit that did not lose a drop. He recalled having studied together with him in *cheder*. When Rabbi Eliyahu was a mere four years old, so they used to tell in Vilkamir, the *rebbe* asked him to note the differences in the Ten Commandments as they appeared in *Yisro* which they had studied the previous year, and as they were brought in *Va'eschanan*, which they were studying at the present. The child did not hesitate long before enumerating all the variances, such as "*zachor*" in the one and "*shamor*" in the other; "*lo sachmod*" in one and "*lo tisaveh*" in the other, and so forth. The *melamed* was astounded at the child's memory and kissed him upon the forehead.

The righteous Reb Shmuel Shenker used to tell a story told to him by his father, the eminent Rabbi Avraham Tanis. The *melamed* once asked his young charges how many times the word ladder, *sulam*, was mentioned throughout the twenty-four books of *Tanach*. Five-year-old Eliyahu jumped up with a ready reply, "The only time we find that word in the entire *Tanach* is in P*arshas Vayeitzei*."

Rabbi Yisrael Buria had also heard a vignette from his

father, a *cheder*-mate of Rabbi Eliyahu's. The Grodna milkman, who delivered to Rabbi Eliyahu's house each day, would mark down his tally in chalk on a blackboard by the sink. One day, someone inadvertently wiped it off.

"What a terrible thing!" exclaimed Eliyahu's father. "How will I know how much I owe the milkman? Heaven save me from being guilty of stealing from him!"

Little Eliyahu heard his sigh and piped up, "Don't worry, Father. I clearly remember the figures written on the board." And without delay, he ran over to the blackboard and wrote down the numbers just as they had appeared before, to everyone's amazement.

The people of Yerushalayim could go on and with similar tales about Rabbi Eliyahu Meir.

In Meah Shearim, Rabbi Eliyahu Meir seemed like a simple Jew, naively wholesome and upright, whose piety surpassed his knowledge; he prayed at length, completing the entire *Tehillim* each day, fasted continually and made it his practice to gaze upon the Brisker Rav's face every single day.

Actually, all this was a mere carryover from Grodna, where rather than flaunt his wisdom, he had undertaken the menial duties of *shamash* in the city's central *beis knesses*. The work was, literally, *shamash*-work, such as scrubbing floors, arranging books, aligning chairs, preparing candles, spreading tablecloths over the tables, collecting pledges. All this in return for the pittance that was enough for his family to subsist upon.

He served at this post during the lifetime of Rav Binyamin Diskin, Rabbi of Grodna, even before the birth of the present Brisker Rav, Rav Yehoshua Leib, and continued at it until he was well on in years. When he saw that he was enjoying a full complement of years, he made an oath to ascend to Yerushalayim and dedicate his last years to Torah and prayer. He had now fulfilled this promise.

One day, about a month after he arrived, the Brisker Rav summoned Rabbi Eliyahu to his private study and there begged his forgiveness for a slight he had inflicted upon him as a child in Grodna, while his father, Rav Binyamin had been alive.

Rabbi Eliyahu Meir was appalled at the very idea that such a great man need ask his forgiveness. His bones knocked together in fearful awe before the saintly figure of the *gaon* and without even knowing at first what was being alluded to, he quickly replied, "I forgive, I forgive . . ."

The *gaon's talmidim* stood by the door, wondering at the exchange inside of which they knew nothing, though they clearly heard the elderly Rabbi Eliyahu's swift, "*Machul lo*, I forgive!" As soon as he emerged, they swooped down upon the old man and one of them, the favored Rav Yaakov Orenstein, begged that he divulge the contents of the conversation and explain the *gaon's* apology.

At first, Rabbi Eliyahu refused to discuss the matter at all, but the disciples would not desist. They coaxed the old man into the nearby Ohel Moshe *yeshivah*, sat him at the table and finally, after much insistent pleading, succeeded in extracting the story from his reluctant lips.

"When I was a young man in Grodna," Rabbi Eliyahu began his tale, "I served as *shamash* in Rav Binyamin Diskin's *beis midrash*. Since this work did not suffice to support me, I sought various sidelines. From time to time, I would sell raffles for various objects of value and this income eased my situation somewhat.

"Once, before *Chanukah*, I bought a silver *menorah* to raffle off. I labored hard for an entire month, selling the hundred half-ruble tickets to the members of the *shul*. I finally managed to sell them all.

"On the day of the drawing, after *Shacharis*, I prepared a ballot box in the hallway. All the children of the city gathered to watch while I deposited one hundred tickets with one hundred different numbers, shook them up inside, then called one of the boys to draw the winning ticket. It happened to be number eighteen, *chai*. Noticing the owner of the ticket still in *shul*, I immediately gave him his prize, the silver *menorah*, along with my congratulations. And that was that.

"Now that the drawing was completed, the children felt free to seize the ballot box, overturning it so that the tickets were strewn all over the floor. And as children will, they replayed the lottery as a game, calling out all the numbers aloud.

"In the course of their play it was discovered that the number fourteen appeared twice. Little Yehoshua Leib called out, 'Ahh! The lottery is disqualified!' When the children did not understand, he turned to the adults who stood nearby, to have them invalidate the lottery. The adults rejected his claim, saying that the double number did not disqualify the drawing. If number fourteen had been drawn, one might have argued that the owner of that particular number had had a double chance of winning over the other participants since he, too, had only paid a half-ruble into the pot. But since that number had not been drawn, the adults explained, it made no difference either way.

"Little Yehoshua Leib would not accept their reasoning and continued to insist that the drawing was unfair. In the midst of the argument, his father Rav Binyamin arrived to give his daily lecture in *Shulchan Aruch*. When he heard the child arguing with men far older than he, he inquired into the cause of the controversy. One of the elder congregants explained the matter.

Rav Binyamin, who was well aware of his son's perspicacity, called the child over and asked to hear his view. The child stood up on a bench and began speaking.

"'What would have happened if number fourteen had been drawn? You would have disclaimed the lottery for the simple reason that the owner of the ticket had had an additional chance of winning. We see, therefore, that the holder of ticket number fourteen was automatically disqualified from this drawing due to the double appearance of his number and could not possibly have won the prize, under any circumstances, even though he gave his half-ruble like everyone else. If, on the other hand, Rabbi Eliyahu Meir had left out a number, you would surely concede that the drawing was invalid. Why is this case any different?'

"Everyone was amazed at the child's logical analysis and agreed that he was right. I then had to make another drawing, even though I had already awarded the prize to one of the city's respected congregants, his number having been picked in the original drawing. This brought the matter to a close."

Now, some seventy years since that incident in the Grodna *shul*, Rav Yehoshua Leib had summoned the *shamash* to his home in Yerushalayim to apologize for having caused him inconvenience. The city was overwhelmed.

The Bookbinder's Marriage

Being offered a seat by Rav Yehoshua Leib Diskin was an almost unheard of and cherished honor in the eyes of Yerushalayim Jewry. Anyone thus honored by the Brisker Rav likewise acquired the respect of the local people. Yerushalayim's

Jews held the Brisker Rav in their highest esteem; they regarded him with an exalted love from the day he set foot in their city. And even the slightest look, the merest glance from his holy eyes, set the trend for the whole city.

Yerushalayim's Jews were one big family in those days. The community was prodigious in quality, but tiny in quantity. Hate and jealously did not even exist. All were equally poor, equally immersed in Torah study and the pursuit of *mitzvos*, young as well as old. Each person was subservient to his neighbor and all subservient to the Torah giants who were their leaders.

They celebrated their *simchos* together, whether *bris, bar-mitzvah* or marriage. All were invited to participate, and all rejoiced equally with a new soul, or at a marriage—on Friday afternoons in most cases—which took place in the combined homes of adjacent neighbors.

The Yerushalayim Jews did not come to indulge themselves in fat dinners; they were not offered any to begin with. Each wedding had a standard menu.

There was, however, one wedding that proved to be an exception, and it became the talk of the town. This was Manish the bookbinder's wedding.

Why was this wedding so unusual? Who was Manish the bookbinder?

It all started with the slight hint that Rav Yehoshua Leib Diskin dropped to the *gabbai* of the Kerem *shul*, Reb Zimmel, implying that participation in the bookbinder's wedding was singularly important.

"Well," the disciples of the Brisker Rav said, "if Reb Zimmel, a man so close to the Brisker Rav, says that the *rav* hinted thus, then there is no reason to doubt his words." Reb Zimmel was an honest man who lived by the sweat of his brow

24

even while dedicating most of his days to Torah and prayer. His four sons-in-law, choice young scholars in Yerushalayim *yeshivos*, were all supported by him.

Manish's wedding took place in the Kerem section of Yerushalayim where his elderly parents lived. His father was long since bedridden with disease, and his mother crippled by the whip of a Turkish porter on the very day she set foot on holy soil. It was celebrated on one of the shorter Friday afternoons in *Teves* and, although the weather itself was warm and pleasant, the roads were muddy. This did not deter people from attending, however, and wagonload after wagonload arrived from the Old City to the neighborhood outside the walls, spewing forth an enormous crowd of people. Among these were the majority of Yerushalayim's elite. Rav Yosef Chaim Sonnenfeld, the *mesader kiddushin*, was accompanied by his son, Reb Avraham Aharon. Rabbi Yissachar Dov Zwebner, son of Rav Avraham Shag, with his wife, were honored with leading the bridal couple to the *chuppah*. Rabbi Zevulun Charlap of the Brisker Rav's *beis din* was present, as were Reb Zerach Braverman, Rav Nota Tzvi Weiss, the famous *maggid,* Reb Zalman Baharan and his brothers Rav David, Rav Shalom Pester and many others.

The carriage bearing the *kallah*, Zlata, the niece of Reb Moshe Shochet Frankenthal, who was one of the chief disciples of the Brisker Rav, arrived. The same carriage brought the Brisker Rebbetzin, Rav Shmuel Salant's respected wife, the wife of the famed Reb Shneur Zalman of Lublin, Mattel Biderman, wife of Reb Dovid'l and Rebbetzin Sherel Sonnenfeld. Other worthy women also appeared, loaded down with heavy baskets full of jars of herring pickled especially for the wedding feast and decorated with lemon slices and bay leaves, with cakes, pastries and bagels that had shared the oven with *Shabbos challos*. The good women also brought a large barrel of aged wine that had been collectively donated by families in the Old City, and pillowcases full of sunflower seeds, chick peas and nuts.

The square in front of the synagogue filled, and the crowd expanded tidally from minute to minute into a sea of *shtreimels*, crowding up front as if each were the *chasan's* closest relative. As the sun began its descent from the treetops, Reb Zimmel hurried the last minute preparations. A gold and silver embroidered *chuppah* was lifted over the heads of the *chasan* and his attendants. The *kallah* was led under it. Then Rav Chaim Sonnenfeld began the ceremony.

Why did the Brisker Rav see fit to invite, almost summon, Yerushalayim's elite to this wedding of a simple bookbinder of nineteen? Why did he deem it necessary to assemble these men and women on the shortest of Fridays in the midst of their hurried *Shabbos* preparations?

No one knew. A small group, however, were fortunate enough that *Shabbos* evening after *maariv*, to hear Reb Avraham Aharon Sonnenfeld explain the event.

"It began on the twenty-first of *Iyar* in the year 5633, thirty years ago," began Reb Avraham Aharon. "That was when my father arrived in Yerushalayim, accompanying his *rebbe*, the famous Rav Avraham Shag of Kobersdorf. My father was only twenty-four years old then, and the Jewish community was in the beginning of its development. The Batei Machseh section, which had just been completed a short while before, was the only Jewish neighborhood at the time, except for the few scattered Jewish homes, built among the Arab dwellers. Any Jew who left his homeland in Europe in order to settle in Yerushalayim could expect only hardship and suffering before he found a safe haven he could call home.

"The good people of Kobersdorf were well aware of this problem and had made provisions beforehand for their esteemed *rav*. When he arrived in Yerushalayim there was a small apartment waiting for him in Batei Machseh. Not so my father, who was so humble and retiring that no one even knew that he intended to go to Yerushalayim together with his *rebbe* until he set foot on ship's deck. Since no living quarters had been prepared for him, he was forced to spend several nights under the cover of the Yerushalayim sky. My mother joked about her plight then, saying that she had expected to lived in "Batei Machseh," the House of Shelter, and found that she had neither a house nor a shelter. Rav Avraham Shag was deeply distressed about the situation, but there was nothing that he could do.

"Rav Avraham Shag had a neighbor who was also distressed by the fact that the young man and his wife had no roof over their heads. Reb Noach Yudel, originally from Dvinsk and a carpenter by profession, took the problem to heart and decided to do something about it. This Reb Yudel was no simple man. Throughout the many years that he had lived in Yerushalayim he had been active in communal affairs. He had, in addition, built a *shtender* for the renowned Rav Nachum Levi of Shadik on which that *rav* had studied throughout the years. He had designed and executed the new *bimah* in the large Churva *shul*, and he had crafted the huge carved doors of the Misgav Ladach Hospital.

"The name he made for himself as a craftsman was surpassed only by the good name he acquired for his integrity and good heart. Reb Yudel applied his trade for four hours daily, dedicating the remainder of the day to study and prayer. He kept his mouth closed, fleeing from any hint of forbidden speech. His lips formed only holy words; going and coming from his workshop, they moved constantly in prayer and study.

"Reb Yudel divined the hidden treasure in Rav Avraham's modest disciple. Seeing that the young man had no place to call home and no money to enable him to acquire such a place, he resolved to do something about the situation. Reb Yudel was the kind of man who, having once decided that something must be done, does not rest until that thing is done. Within three days, he found a small flat in an Arab building, paid two months' rent in advance and furnished the humble abode with a table and chairs of his own making. It was then all ready for my father to inhabit it, which the young man and his wife gratefully did.

"Rav Avraham Shag, learning of Reb Yudel's dedicated effort on behalf of his disciple, went to the carpenter to thank him personally and to let him know something about the object of his kindness. 'You have prepared a home for a great light which will soon illuminate the skies of the Holy Land. Surely this great merit will stand you in good stead for the rest of your life,' Rav Avraham told the carpenter as he stood on the threshold of his neighbor's house.

"Rav Avraham turned to go, but the carpenter barred his way and burst into tears. 'Rabbi, if I indeed performed an act of merit, then I did so without realizing the true value of your disciple and without expecting gain of any kind. Therefore, for the sake of this *mitzvah*, I beg you, please bless me with children.'

"Reb Yudel tried to hold back his torrent of tears as he provided some background to his tragedy. 'I have been married for twenty years already, *rebbe*.' He added that a celebrated Viennese doctor had recently visited Yerushalayim and had told the couple that there was no hope for them. Reb Yudel's wife

28

was in the next room, and Rav Avraham could hear her sobs as her husband presented his request.

"The *tzaddik* from Kobersdorf thought for a short while, his face aglow and his eyes assuming a strange cast. Then he suddenly promised Reb Yudel that he and his wife would be truly blessed with a son in the course of the coming year.

"The year had not yet completed its cycle when his blessing was realized, and the middle-aged couple celebrated the birth of their newborn son. His *bris* was celebrated on *erev Pesach* of the year 5634 in the Batei Machseh synagogue. Rav Avraham Shag was honored as *sandak*, and my father was the *mohel*. The boy born twenty-one years after Reb Yudel's marriage was named Manish, after his grandfather, Reb Manish Aidels, who had belonged to the inner circle of the Vilna Gaon's disciples. A huge feast celebrated the occasion, in which all of the important people of Yerushalayim participated and, true to his character, Reb Yudel set aside one table on the eastern wall and had it heaped lavishly with good food for all the poor people of the city.

"Reb Yudel and his wife had hoped to entrust the boy to Rav Avraham's tutelage, but that great man departed this world when Manish was a child of not yet three. And strangely enough, Reb Yudel was forewarned of the *tzaddik's* death.

"It happened on a Friday evening, on the twenty-eighth of *Adar*, 5636, after Reb Yudel had just finished his *Shabbos* meal. He fully intended to go to Rav Meir Auerbach's home for that Rav from Kalish, famed author of *Imrei Binah*, customarily expounded on Torah thoughts and *mussar* ideas from the weekly portion before a huge crowd. Reb Yudel finished *birchas hamazon* and was on the verge of leaving when he was overtaken by a heavy slumber. In this deep sleep he dreamed he

29

saw one of the ancient and cherished Torah scrolls in the ark of the Batei Machseh *shul* burning, G-d forbid. He awoke in a fright. But the dreadful dream did not deter him from rushing to the home of the Kalisher Rav.

"Reb Yudel had not missed the lecture. When it was over, and the people began to return to their respective homes, Reb Yudel approached the *rav* and repeated his frightening dream. The *rav* listened in fear and then told Reb Yudel how to observe the *halachah* about fasting for a bad dream on *Shabbos*.

"By the following morning the news was all over the city; Rav Avraham Shag had been summoned to the heavenly realms. The matter was discussed at the Rav of Kalish's *Shabbos* table that day. One of his disciples remarked how strange it was that an event of such moment to the Jewish community should have been revealed beforehand to a mere carpenter. But the *rav* answered shortly, 'Simple wooden vessels do not absorb *tumah*.'

"A year passed and Manish began *cheder*. His father borrowed the *tallis* that had belonged to Rav Avraham Shag for the momentous occasion and, wrapped up in that holy garment, the boy was brought to commence his Torah education at the Eitz Chaim *cheder*.

"The lad excelled and was promoted from class to class with a rapidity that astounded his teachers. The years sped by, years full of *nachas* for the elderly parents. On one occasion, Reb Yudel met Rav Eliezer Dan Ralbag on the street and the latter related in glowing terms that he had tested the boy's knowledge just that week, and Manish excelled in understanding and erudition. On the next day, Reb Dovid'l Biderman stopped the carpenter in the marketplace and also spoke highly about the boy's piety in prayer and general enthusiasm for *mitzvos*.

"Although his parents pinned great hopes upon their only

son, Manish did not succeed in fulfilling them all. Before he became seventeen, Manish's father became paralyzed and bedridden. His crippled mother, likewise, soon took to her bed. There was no choice but for Manish to seek some way to support the family and, knowing that his parents' lives were at stake, he did not hesitate long. Within a month he had learned bookbinding, rented a tiny shop on Jews' Street and hung out his shingle.

"He worked diligently but earned sparingly. No wonder, for he spent most of his days studying; his profession was only incidental. He did not leave his learning partners, never missing a *shiur* in the *yeshivah* or a session with his close friend Yeshaya Cheshin, his learning partner of many years' standing."

"The store had been open for business for about two weeks when the Brisker Rav happened to pass by, accompanied by a train of disciples. Noticing the modest new shop, he asked his disciples about it and was informed about the owner by Reb Yitzchak Shlomo Blau, who knew about the young Manish who had been forced to turn his hand to a livelihood. To the great surprise of all his *talmidim*, the *rav* stepped into the tiny shop. He found Manish in the midst of his work. When the young lad looked up and saw the Brisker Rav standing before him in his own shop, he nearly fainted. His tools fell out of his trembling hands, his voice stuck momentarily in his throat. Then he arose.

"'*Rebbe* . . .' he said in a voice filled with humility, 'I have opened a bookbinding store here . . . p-please bless me.'

"The Brisker Rav stretched out his hand to the lad. 'My son, beware of taking in secular books by "progressive" and atheistic writers. If you are careful, the labor of your hands will be blessed.' His *talmidim* heard his words and quickly answered, '*Vihi noam*—May the pleasure of Hashem be upon us and the labor of our hands . . .'

31

"The *rav* and his entourage left the store and continued on their way, leaving Manish stunned by the surprise visit of the great man to his tiny shop. And little wonder! Even great men proudly boasted when the Brisker Rav spoke only one or two words to them, while Manish could claim a personal visit!

"'Who am I and what am I that I have merited this?' he murmured to himself. That was the end of work for Manish that day. Instead, he spent the remainder in repentance and prayer hoping that Heaven would assist him in heeding the *rav's* exhortation. And from that day on, when Manish opened his shop in the morning, he would stop at the *mezuzah* on the doorpost and offer a short prayer, '*Ribono Shel Olam*, this humble being prostrated itself before You in a plea. Don't let me, G-d forbid, stumble in my work and unknowingly transgress the ban on binding a suspicious book...' Only then would he proceed to his daily work, ignoring the tiny tears that invariably formed in his eyes.

"Days passed and the *rav's* visit, which had been the talk of all Yerushalayim, was forgotten. Manish, meanwhile, had acquired a name as being an accomplished tradesman. The Jews of Yerushalayim put their trust in his craftsmanship, and he did not lack business.

"'It was not an unattainable ideal,' Reb Leibush Weber would say, pointing to Manish as his perfect example, 'to fulfill the words of the *Mesillas Yesharim* that 'one can be a true *chassid* even if circumstances force one to perform simple labor.'

"Seated at his workbench, sewing, pasting, aligning pages and being totally involved in his work, Manish could be heard murmuring a half-silent prayer, 'My Father in heaven, I, Manish the son of Miriam Devorah, beseech you to save me from having a forbidden book find its way to my shop . . . Oh, *Ribono Shel Olam*, help me fulfill what is written in Your Torah, "How shall youth justify his path to persevere in Your commands."'

"The truth was that Manish would not have recognized a forbidden book if he had held one between his hands. He knew about Torah, *Nevi'im* and *Kesuvim*. He knew about *Shas* and *poskim*. But what kind of books did heretics write? He could not fathom. He had heard denunciations, upon the several occasions when *mussar* lecturers had visited the *yeshivah*, of '*bichelach*' and newspapers. He had seen these denunciations reinforced in sacred *sefarim*, But that a questionable book should actually find its way into the Holy City of Yerushalayim—that was something he could not even imagine possible!

"No wonder then, that worry gnawed inside him. Who knows, he fretted, if I have not at some time inadvertently bound forbidden books without even being aware of it? He had even heard his teacher, Rav Eliezer Dan Ralbag, reveal that there were some Jews sporting long beards and worthy deeds who had been ensnared by progressiveness. Maybe, thought Manish, I would be better off finding some different occupation altogether, something that is free from pitfalls and consequently not as dangerous.

"It happened once, during the *bein hamitzarim* period, the three-week interval between the two fast days commemorating the destruction of the *Beis Hamikdash*, that Manish was subjected to temptation in the very area he feared. He used to close his shop before noon during those introspective days in order to join the worshippers at the Mechavnim Shul in reciting the *tikun chatzos* in the daytime. Just as he was locking up one day, an honored client entered. It was the *tzaddik* Reb Mesher Gelbstein, who had come to bind a *Chidushei Harim*, which had just been sent to him from Warsaw where it had been published.

"Manish took this opportune moment to bare his problem to the saintly man. Reb Meshel heard the youth's conflict and sighed, 'You have touched upon a serious problem, my son, one which must really be posed to a qualified rabbi. You cannot rely on your own judgment in this matter; it is like playing with fire.'

"At that moment, they heard the *shamash* of the *Chevra Kadisha* announcing the death of Rav Mordechai Eliezer Weber, the zealous *Rav* of Oda. Reb Meshel ran outside and prodded the bookbinder to follow suit. 'A great man has left us. All work must cease.' Reb Meshel proceeded to the funeral, followed by Manish. On their way they met Rav Akiva Yosef Schlesinger, author of *Lev Ha-ivri*, and Reb Meshel remembered Manish's question. He grabbed the youth's hand and led him to Rav Akiva Yosef, saying, 'Here is your qualified rabbi. He will be able to direct you in your work.'

"Reb Meshel then explained the young bookbinder's dilemma to Rav Akiva Yosef and, vouching for the young tradesman, begged him to direct the youth. Rav Akiva Yosef thought about it for a short while and then agreed. Manish felt deeply relieved and would have danced for joy had he not been at a funeral, for a heavy burden had been rolled off his heart.

"From that day on, Manish did not bind any book before it had gone through the critical hands of Rav Akiva Yosef. There was just one drawback. Since his new critic tended to judge books rather harshly, Manish's business was diminished by half. Who, in the Yerushalayim of then, had the money to spend on binding books anyway, if not for progressive men like Pines, Yellin and their ilk, the representatives of Chovevei Zion? They could afford to bind their books lavishly, too, in leather and cloth with gold letters—work that they paid generously for.

"Manish's circumstances grew increasingly difficult. After the monthly allotment he gave his parents, he barely had a few coins left to live on himself. For a long period, all Manish ate was dark bread with a little sesame oil that he bought from the Arabs. His neighbors in the Kerem section testified that not a drop of milk entered his lips for months at a time. But nothing could allay his happiness in having found, through G-d's kind help, a patron who supervised his work and kept him from stumbling through ignorance into error."

At this point, Reb Avraham Aharon's listeners interrupted his story. "All right, so Manish is a singularly G-d-fearing young man. But all he is, in the end, is a mere bookbinder. How did he become the husband of the famous Reb Moshe Frankenthal's niece, a *tzaddekes* in her right, famed throughout the city for her character and good deeds? Is there such a dearth of *talmidei chachamim* that this particular young man was chosen as her partner?"

Reb Avraham Aharon heard their comments but did not react. He merely continued the thread of the story.

"One day as Manish was working at his books, a Yemenite Jew stopped in front of the store and began unloading a heavily-laden donkey. He untied bundle after bundle of books and handed five gold coins to Manish. Such a sum was enough to support an entire family for a whole month! What's more, he promised the young bookbinder, in the name of his employer, that if the books were bound well he would receive further payment.

"Manish was at a loss as to what to do. Indeed, the fat down payment and the huge array of books seemed very suspicious to him, and he wanted to stop the Jew from unloading the bundles then and there. But he was loathe to bother a worker who had labored so much already simply on the chance that these books were questionable. Fortunately, at that moment, Reb Moshe Frankenthal happened to pass by and Manish pounced on him happily and dragged him inside. Reb Moshe let himself be led by the insistent bookbinder. He took one of the books into his hands and it fell open to the title page, '*Children of My Spirit*, by Michel Pines,'. Reb Moshe, thoroughly agitated, threw the book away. It was heretical through and through. Manish didn't need to be told anything more explicit than that; he immediately told the Yemenite Jew to take his merchandise back where it came from. Returning the five gold pieces, and adding a few coins for the man's labors, Manish began to reload the donkey and then accompanied them a few steps despite the Yemenite Jew's protests.

"'My employer is a Jew with a long beard. He wears a rabbinical coat. What could be wrong with these books?' the Yemenite wondered. But Manish persisted and sent the man on his way.

"Reb Moshe was deeply impressed by the youth's righteousness and at the wellspring of strength inside him that enabled him to withstand such temptation in his circumstances of poverty. He decided then and there to have the boy marry his renowned and excellent niece and spoke to the girl's father that very day. Rav Yaakov Orenstein took his brother-in-law's word as to the bookbinder's suitability and the match was confirmed."

It was no idle rumor, the disciples of the Brisker Rav finally agreed, when Reb Zimmel said that the great *rav* had hinted at the importance of participating in this wedding. His disciples now understood as well why the wedding had been graced by the two-hour-long dancing of three Yerushalayim celebrities,

Rav Eliezer Dan Ralbag, Reb Yaakov Blumenthal and Reb Tuvya Goldberger. Who could hear their ecstatic singing of "*Yibaneh*—let the *Beis Hamikdash* be rebuilt and the city of Zion filled" without joining fervently?

The Lost *Yarmulka*

"Yerushalayim kneels under its yoke of suffering. Disease runs rampant. Hunger daily reaps its harvest in souls. Infants cry out for bread but receive no reply. Cholera strikes out at young and old alike. We have no one to turn to except our Father in heaven."

A Yerushalayim resident thus described the situation in the city in a letter to a Polish relative in the year 5676. And yet, on one of these difficult days when everyone was concerned and anxious to still the hunger pangs of his own family or to supply a cup of brackish water to unfortunates hovering between life and death, a strange sight drew people's attention. It was Reb Yona Lefkowitz, devoted *talmid* and aid of Reb Yosef of Poppah, hurrying through the city streets, clutching a parcel of notices in one hand and a pot of home-made flour paste in the other, pasting up announcements in the hallways and on the bulletin boards of the synagogues and *batei midrash* of the Old City.

The notices themselves did not arouse any interest. The bulletin boards were already replete with numerous announcements—calls for women to strengthen their practice of modesty, warnings to refrain from *lashon hora* and general pleas for repentance. Thus, the small notices which Reb Yona now posted did not stand out at all, in fact they were "nullified in sixty" among the rest. It was Reb Yona's faithfulness and alacrity in performing the act itself that drew people's attention.

A brief inquiry revealed that it was Reb Yona's *rebbe*, Reb Zerach Braverman, who had entrusted him with this responsibility. People now crowded around to read the interesting communication which one of the Torah leaders and foremost figures of *chesed* in Yerushalayim had directed to be posted, and this by one of Yerushalayim's noble souls. The notes read as follows:

> LOST: I have lost a *yarmulka*. It's identifying signs are: it is worn out and has a hole along its side. Whoever finds it is requested to kindly return it to me at the first opportunity. He will thus be fulfilling the *mitzvah* of returning lost property.
>
> (Signed) Zerach Braverman

Reb Dan Hochheiser, male nurse, stood by the public bulletin board at the gate of the Misgav Ladach Hospital and read the brief message. With a slighting motion towards his head, he remarked bitterly, "The *yarmulka* itself is not worth a farthing. It would not even fetch the price of half a cup of clear water. Yet Reb Zerach is concerned with such inanities. Have we reached such a state of affairs because of our many troubles?" His face grew serious.

Kasriel Tweed, gateman of the hospital, had meanwhile joined Reb Dan as the second reader of the note. His reaction was similar. "I cannot understand Reb Zerach. He is known to be a clever and righteous person. Has he no concern, in these days when the cemeteries continually fill up with fresh corpses and the hospitals with the victims of starvation, other than the loss of a worn out *yarmulka*? Why, the very pennies he laid out for the notes and the paste could have been spared for a better purpose in these demented times!"

"Be silent. Refrain from finding fault with Reb Zerach," Reb Yosef Binyamin Shimanowitz, the *shochet* who had come to visit his sick daughter, silenced them. "One must judge even a common person in the market favorably. All the more so, a *gaon* and *tzaddik* such as Reb Zerach! If he is so concerned about an old *yarmulka*, certainly he has a particular interest in it."

Two weeks passed, but the *yarmulka* was not found. The *kipah* was gone and Reb Zerach mourned it as if he had lost a precious pearl. Seeing his distress and anguish over the loss, his neighbor, Reb Avraham Yochanan Blumenthal naively went to buy a new one from the righteous Sheindel Blau, mother of the Blau brothers who used to spin the thread herself, reciting a chapter of *Tehillim* after each row of knitting. He presented the gift to Reb Zerach.

"A Jew like yourself should not be so disconsolate over such an insignificant item," he told Reb Zerach.

"I am amazed at you," Reb Zerach countered. "Did you really think that I was upset over the loss of just a plain *yarmulka*? Don't you know that I have a wealth of *kipos* in my house? It is a specific *yarmulka* whose loss grieves me."

The Admor, Reb David'l Biderman, who had always amazed Reb Zerach with his trait of truthfulness, had also come across the note stuck on the board of his *beis midrash*, had read it and commented, "I am certain that if Reb Zerach is searching for a lost *yarmulka* in such times he surely has a special reason for doing so. I am equally sure that it will be returned to him in the near future."

Another two weeks passed by. Suddenly, one evening,

Salem the Arab painter who had been hired just before *Pesach* to whitewash the rabbi's house, appeared at Reb Zerach's house, the *yarmulka* in hand. Apologizing profusely, he explained that in the course of his work in Reb Zerach's home he had noticed a copper case in the closet, and thinking that it contained some item of value, he had stolen it. When he had later opened the case at home and had found nothing more than a worn and torn *yarmulka*, he had angrily thrown the case and *kipah* into his cellar, promptly forgetting about the entire incident.

The Arab paused briefly, then continued. "Today I was hired to paint Reb David'l Biderman's house. While I was standing high on my ladder, painting the ceiling, the *chacham* suddenly entered the room and began shaking the ladder until I almost fell off. He looked up at me and said, 'Salem, does the Moslem religion allow you to steal?'

"These words penetrated deep into my heart like a sharpened arrow. I was convinced that the *chacham* was addressing me with truly prophetic words. I decided to immediately go home and return the stolen property to its owner."

The Arab finished his tale and retreated shamefacedly. Reb Zerach's eyes, meanwhile, had filled with tears which overflowed, wetting the coveted, worn, torn *yarmulka*.

Reb Yechiel Michel Tikochinsky, *rosh yeshivah* at the Eitz Chaim *yeshivah*, heard the story and noted, "I am surprised at Reb David'l for having used Divine intuition for the sake of a used *yarmulka*."

And what, indeed, was the secret, the significance, of this *kipah* which occupied the interest of many of Yerushalayim's famous figures during the span of several weeks?

Thirty years before, when Reb Leib Chafetz had taken ill,

his *rebbe*, the Gaon of Brisk, Rav Yehoshua Leib Diskin, had removed his *kipah* from his head and had it sent by messenger to Reb Leib.

The messenger had been young Moishele Blau who later grew up to become one of the leaders of Orthodox Jewry. By the time the boy reached his destination, Reb Leib had already returned his soul to his Maker. The intelligent child refused to go back to the Gaon of Brisk with the news of his favorite *talmid's* death. Instead, he returned to his *cheder*, crushed and broken in spirit. Reb Avraham Aharon Prague, his *rebbe* at the Shomrei Hachomos *cheder* asked him about the strange article he clutched, and the boy told the story between sobs.

"Do not be distressed, my child," Reb Avraham Aharon comforted his young student. "This *kipah* worn by the Gaon of Brisk assuredly has the power to perform many marvels. Time will yet tell . . ."

Reb Leib Chafetz's funeral took place that very day. The Gaon of Brisk participated in it. The child realized that he would be able to return the *kipah* to its rightful owner at that occasion. When he brought it, Rav Yehoshua Leib Diskin was flanked by Reb Zerach Braverman. The Gaon of Brisk lifted the *yarmulka* and said, "Reb Zerach, I am giving you this *yarmulka* for safekeeping."

Reb Zerach took the headgear, not daring to inquire about it or the task he had been entrusted with. From that time on, the *kipah* remained in his possession, encased in a copper container. It was not removed for years. When the First World War broke out, Reb Ben Zion, son of Reb Tzvi Michel became very ill. His condition worsened until signs of approaching death became evident. The members of his family ran hither and thither to all the great men of Yerushalayim to solicit their prayers on his behalf. Reb Zerach then removed the *kipah* from its receptacle and went himself to Reb Ben Zion, placing it on his head. Within a short interval the sick man's condition had noticeably improved.

The righteous doctor, Reb Moshe Wallach, who had stood guard by the bedside of the patient for many hours of the day, was thoroughly aroused. "A worn out *kipah* belonging to the *Gaon* of Brisk has greater healing powers than all the medicines in the world!" he exclaimed.

It is not difficult, therefore, to understand why Reb Zerach had been so distressed over the loss of that *kipah*—and so relieved and joyful when it was returned to him.

The Tombstone Engraver

On the third of *Kislev*, 5657, an elderly woman stood on the Jaffa dock, waving to her husband seated in the rowboat that would convey him to the ship about to sail abroad. Bystanders could not help being curious at the spectacle before them. What possible fortune could this elderly man be seeking in the Diaspora during the few years left him? Surely he must have suffered enough in just reaching these blessed shores! Why was he leaving them?

Wednesday, the second day of *Kislev*. The year, 5568. The Rabbi of Brisk, Rabbi Chaim Soloveichik, stood on the steps of the *aron kodesh* in the central synagogue in Brisk, amid the huge crowd that had gathered to hear Rabbi Avraham of Yaleikovsky.

Suddenly, there was commotion and alarm. One of the assembled, a stranger to the city, had fainted. Only Rav Chaim could identify the man as the Yerushalayim *meshulach*, Reb

Zusman Vasher, who lived in Meah Shearim where he maintained a small monument shop but who had now found his way to Brisk.

Still unconscious, Reb Zusman was taken to his lodgings at the home of Rabbi Simcha Zelig Riger, well known *halachic* authority in Brisk. After much labor and effort, Dr. Ganichovsky managed to revive him but before long, the stranger had fainted again. The scene was repeated four or five times, the doctor making all efforts to revive the man, only to have the patient collapse soon after. Finally, however, his efforts succeeded.

What was the cause of his fainting? Weakness? Exhaustion? The doctor determined otherwise. Despite his age, Reb Zusman Vasher was known to be healthy, robust and vigorous, having been sick only once in his life.

"Some worry must be disturbing him," Rabbi Simcha Zelig concluded.

What, indeed, had prompted Reb Zusman Vasher to leave his wife, his city Yerushalayim, where he had been living for years, his store and his *shchunah* of Meah Shearim which he loved wholeheartedly, to voyage to the Diaspora? And why to Brisk, of all places?

Born in Slonim, Reb Zusman was orphaned at the age of five when both his father and mother were killed in a tragic fire that broke out in their home. He was then taken to Brisk by his uncle, the great Rabbi Simcha Zelig Riger, who brought him up as a son.

After he married, Reb Zusman opened a laundry business in the Jewish market square. This provided him with only a meager livelihood since he continued to make Torah study his prime concern to which business was only secondary. When Rav Yehoshua Leib Diskin of Brisk decided to emigrate to Eretz

43

Yisrael in 5637, he was inspired to follow suit. Rabbi Simcha Zelig encouraged Reb Zusman to take the decisive step. In 5639, he and his wife reached Eretz Yisrael and rented a small apartment on Chevra Shas Street in the new Meah Shearim section.

Unable to find any means of livelihood—there was no need for a laundry business in the Yerushalayim of yore—Reb Zusman who was skilled with his hands turned to engraving. This occupation provided ample income to allow him to set a fifth of his earning aside each month. This he gave to the Brisker Rav to distribute among the poor.

Reb Zusman made certain to see the Brisker Rav once a day and perform some service for him. If he noticed a broken chair in the house, he would fix it. If the paint was peeling off the walls, he would buy some whitewash and attack the job. Did the *rebbetzin* need an errand? He would run and do it. The main thing was to perform one service, anything of use to the *rav*, every day for this is what his uncle had told him as his parting message. "Gaze upon the Brisker Rav's face each day and you will not be tempted to sin."

In *Tishrei* of 5657, Reb Zusman contracted a severe lung disease. The doctors despaired of his life. His wife Sheindel went to the Brisker Rav's house and stood outside, weeping bitterly, beseeching the *rav* to pray for her husband's recovery. When the *rav* heard the weeping outside his door, he went to the doorway, and standing on the threshold, his eyes shut, he spoke.

"Reb Zusman truly does need a *refuah*, but that has already been prescribed by Heaven. There is no need for despair."

Two days later, Reb Zusman recovered. The *shechunah* was stunned. The young but scholarly Mattisyahu Elba, who was one of the *gabbaim* of the neighborhood, a close friend of Reb

44

Zusman and a relative besides, held a large feast in honor of the occasion.

When he had entirely recuperated, Reb Zusman vowed to go abroad for a full year to raise money for both the Brisker Rav's Diskin Orphanage and the Ohel Moshe *yeshivah*.

Before leaving, he went to the *rav* for a parting blessing. The latter wished him good luck and gave him the *sefer Nefesh Hachaim*, written by Rav Chaim of Volozhin, as "fare" for the way.

"It is difficult to leave you," Reb Zusman confessed to the *rav* before leaving the house. "I have become used to coming here each day and doing something for you. How can I do this if I keep my vow and go abroad?"

"Your mission is a *shlichus mitzvah*. By next *Kislev*, you can be back here in Yerushalayim," replied the Brisker Rav with smiling eyes.

"I am in no rush to perform my holy duty. I am even ready to remain until *Purim*," replied Reb Zusman, warming to the kindliness he saw reflected upon the *gaon's* face.

The *rav* repeated his parting blessing and Reb Zusman left for Brisk, glad to enjoy again the hospitality of his childhood guardian Rabbi Simcha Zelig, who devotedly labored on behalf of Rav Yehoshua's institutions throughout his nephew's stay.

The city of Grabe is quite a distance from Brisk. At the time of our story, the rabbinate there was being filled by Rabbi Avraham Yaleikovsky who was famous for his fiery sermons and his exceptional power to evoke tears and to rouse people to repent.

The Rav of Grabe once returned home from *yeshivah* to find an urgent letter waiting for him from Rav Chaim Soloveichik, Rabbi of Brisk. It asked him to come immediately to Brisk to eulogize the *gadol hador*, Rav Yehoshua Leib Diskin, who had just died in Yerushalayim.

Broken, overwhelmed with the news, the *rav* went to Brisk, overcome with the knowledge that the glorious crown of Israel had fallen. After a full day's voyage by train, he finally arrived in Brisk and in a deep depression, made his way to Rav Chaim's home.

He found Rav Chaim waiting for him at the door. As soon as he entered, Rav Chaim showed him to a seat and began telling him about Rav Yehoshua Leib's greatness, describing his remarkably brilliant mind and his singular saintliness. He spoke for hours on end, beginning with these words.

"Know, worthy Rabbi of Grabe, that before you come to eulogize Rav Yehoshua Leib, you must know all about his personality. Where all words of praise such as *gaon, gadol*, genius leave off, that is where Rav Yehoshua Leib's praises only begin. He was unique in his generation. No one today can compare with him nor can other *tzaddikim* dating several generations back!"

Rav Chaim continued in this vein until near dawn, describing the greatness and saintliness of Rav Yehoshua Leib, coaching the Grabe Rav for his coming *hesped*.

Suddenly, Rav Chaim arose and went to rouse one of the *talmidim* who lodged in his home. He sent him to the *shamash* in the middle of the night to fetch the keys to the large auditorium of the *shul*. The visiting rabbi could not help wondering why Rav Chaim was concerned with those particular keys in the middle of the night! Was the reason important enough for him to wake up a *talmid*? Noting his host's emotional tenseness, he remained silent.

When the *talmid* returned with the key, Rav Chaim told him

to light a candle and lead them to the large *beis knesses*. When the three men were inside the great hall, Rav Chaim asked his guest to walk up to the high *bimah* and rehearse his *hesped*.

The rehearsal was successful.

Rav Chaim's preparations and anxiety over the coming *hesped* affected the Rabbi of Grabe profoundly. He understood that the coming event, which would take place in front of a thousand Brisker residents, was no casual occurrence, especially in Rav Chaim's opinion. Was it any wonder then that he found himself unable to sleep for what remained of the night?

The following day, right after *davening*, town criers circulated throughout Brisk calling upon the entire populace to assemble in the central synagogue for the *maggid's* eulogy bemoaning the Jewish nation's great loss, the passing of Rav Yehoshua Leib Diskin in Yerushalayim.

Thousands of people packed into the *beis knesses*, spilling out to all the neighboring streets. They looked like a sea of heads. Absolute silence reigned when the *rav* arrived together with the visiting Rabbi from Grabe, followed by all the rabbinical figures in the city.

An ocean of tears was spilled during the course of that *hesped*. The wailing did not cease. The Rabbi of Grabe thundered in a mighty voice for three consecutive hours, moving every single heart in the audience.

In the course of his *hesped*, he touched on a story told by our Sages concerning Rabbi Yehuda Hanassi's death. A Heavenly Voice announced at Rebbi's death that whoever had participated in his funeral was assured of entry to the world-to-come. A laundryman, who used to visit the great man's home every day, was out of the city when that precious soul ascended to heaven and deeply regretted it for the rest of his life.

"Would that we, too, had merited participating in the funeral of our saintly rabbi, Rav Yehoshua Leib in Yerushalayim and been among the pallbearers of his sacred bier," he wept.

As soon as these words were out, Reb Zusman Vasher was struck by the thought that they had been directed at him specifically. He collapsed heavily to the ground in a deep faint, half dead and half alive. He was thus transported to his uncle's home where, after considerable effort, he was revived.

When his senses had fully returned, he was approached by Rabbi Simcha Zelig who asked him gently why he had reacted so violently.

Sobbing brokenly, Reb Zusman recalled his parting words to that great personality in Yerushalayim and how the Gaon of Brisk had hinted to him to return home quickly before *Chanukah*. He had not understood the hint and its deeper significance but had in his misguided cleverness decided to remain until the month of *Shevat*. Meanwhile, however, his *rebbe* had ascended to Heaven. He had been robbed of his chance to participate in the *gaon's* funeral.

Reb Zusman continued to weep bitterly and was now joined by Rabbi Simcha Zelig himself who was again struck by the terrible loss that the entire Jewish people had suffered in the spiriting away of this precious jewel.

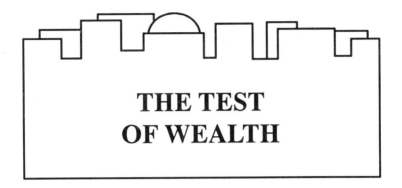

THE TEST
OF WEALTH

A Serious Illness

Numbering among the disciples of Rav Yisrael Salanter, Efraim Nachman Radiner of Toronto was a poor orphan, who not only excelled in Torah and piety but was also a superb craftsman and a *sofer, shochet* and *mohel.*

During a visit to Kovno, one of America's great Jewish industrialists took a deep liking to this talented youth and asked him to be his son-in-law. The marriage took place within a short period. Efraim Nachman moved to America and joined the workers at his father-in-law's plant. Thanks to his gifted hands, he soon gained fame as an inventor of various gadgets and tools. It is even told that when Edison invented his miraculous light-bulb, he was stymied by various technicalities in the practical application of this theory. When he heard of this young man, he enlisted his aid in producing a workable invention.

Efraim Nachman's fame grew from then on. He left his

father-in-law's business and moved to Canada where he established his own factory. His business dealings flourished until within several years, he became one of the world's great millionaires.

It must be said to his credit that despite his vast wealth, Efraim Nachman did not swerve from the pure practice of Judaism. He maintained regular Torah study periods, performed *mitzvos* and gave generously to charitable institutions in Yerushalayim. His acquaintances could testify to the steady monthly tithing of all his profits of which he made precise accounting. At the first opportunity he would send this sum to the rabbis of Jerusalem to be distributed among the city's institutions and poor Torah scholars, as they saw fit.

Efraim Nachman himself visited Yerushalayim several times and from these frequent visits became a close friend of the Yerushalayim leaders who greatly valued his works. He formed close ties with the Gaon of Brisk, Rav Yehoshua Leib Diskin, and with the great Rav Akiva Yosef Schlesinger, in particular.

In 5650, Efraim Nachman became critically ill. As he was sitting at *Shacharis* services in the synagogue, he was suddenly gripped by a coughing attack. When this coughing persisted for many days, he consulted doctors, spending a fortune on the best specialists, but nothing availed. The consensus of the majority of the top experts was that he had developed a hole in his left lung. His days were numbered.

In his distress, Efraim Nachman decided to go to Yerushalayim to pray for his life by the *Kosel* and ask for the blessings of the Jewish leader, the Gaon of Brisk, whom he had respected and admired all these years.

Arriving in Yerushalayim, Efraim Nachman immediately made his way to the home of the Brisker Rav. He would have fallen to the man's feet, begging for his life, had not the great man laid his hand upon Efraim's shoulder. The latter felt an immediate improvement of his symptoms. He actually found it difficult to tell the rabbi of his illness.

But the Brisker Rav did not give him the chance to speak. He turned to him without introduction and said, "Reb Efraim Nachman, you came to Yerushalayim at the right time. Just today a group of communally active people met to formulate a plan whereby sufficient funds could be raised to acquire the lot designated for my orphanage.

"I founded this orphanage," the Gaon of Brisk explained, "to prevent Dr. Herzog from ensnaring Yerushalayim children into the orphanage which he recently established. I pin great hopes upon this institution but the great expense of such an undertaking is prohibitive.

"So you see, Reb Efraim, that you came at exactly the right time."

Reb Efraim Nachman listened to the words, understanding that the great rabbi already knew everything, that the purpose of his visit was evident to him and that he was presenting him with an opportunity to save his life at this very moment. Withdrawing his wallet, he counted out on the table eighteen thousand rubles, which was the full purchase price of the lot and an astronomical sum in those days. The Gaon of Brisk immediately sent a messenger to the home of the Arab owner of the plot, down in the Silwan Valley outside of the city walls. The Arab appeared, the money was transferred to his hands, and the deal was concluded.

Reb Efraim Nachman then sat down before the Rabbi of Brisk, after the great man himself had offered him a seat. He told the Brisker Rav about his serious illness and the physicians' gloomy prognosis that he had no hope for life.

At first, it appeared to Efraim that the great man was preoccupied in his own thoughts and that he was not even listening to his story. But as soon as he had finished his account, the rabbi stood up to his full height and announced, "Listen, my dear Reb Efraim Nachman, our Sages explained the verse, 'And he shall surely heal him,' to concede to the physician divine permission to heal. But from whence comes a physician's sanction to disillusion?"

The Young Messenger

Moishe'le Blau, who later became famous as a leader of devout Jewry in Yerushalayim, was a young lad who had free access to the Brisker Rav's home. His father, the famed Rav Yitzchak Shlomo, who numbered among the *rav's* disciples, used to prompt the lad continually, "Moishele, my son, in your free time between chapters of your lessons by the *melamed*, while your friends are busy playing and running wild, try to be close to the home of the *tzaddik hador*, the great man from Brisk. Perhaps you will be fortunate enough to catch a glimpse of his saintly face. Perhaps you will even be worthy of serving him as a messenger for some service. That will be your merit for immediate *olam haba*."

Moishele followed his father's counsel until his familiarity eventually succeeded in gaining him free access to the *rav's* house. The *rebbetzin* of Brisk, noted for her sagacity, used to befriend Moishele with candies and with the *rav's* raisins.

"This child is extremely wise," she would laud him before his father.

The "Brisker Rav's raisins" were famous in Yerushalayim. They hung in a large bag in a corner of his room. This bag was placed on the *rav's* study table every *Erev Yom Kippur*. He would nibble on these throughout the day to fulfill the rabbinic dictum that "whosoever eats on the ninth is credited with having fasted on both the ninth and tenth [of *Tishrei*]." The raisins were the products of the *rebbetzin's* own hands from the grape season to assure their being free of questionable *orlah* or *kilayim* prohibitions.

Moishele was now summoned to stand before the rabbi. Excited, awestruck, his knees knocking together, he entered the *rav's* study chamber, head bent but eyes turned upward to gaze at the sanctity before him in all its glory. The Gaon of Brisk spoke to him now, for the first time. "Run quickly, my child, to the home of Reb Moshe Jules the medic and tell him to come here immediately."

Little Moishele ran with joy; his feet suddenly became light. Hadn't his father, Rav Yitzchak Shlomo, promised that "perhaps the Gaon of Brisk might avail himself of your services for some errand, that will grant you a sure portion in the world-to-come"? The lad did not tarry for a minute. His friends from *cheder* saw him running with all his might, but he paid them no attention. He reached Reb Moshe Jules' home, fulfilled his errand and his childish heart swelled. He had succeeded this time!

Within a short time, Reb Moshe Jules of the towering stature appeared at the Brisker Rav's home. Reb Moshe had to bend somewhat to avoid bumping his head on the lintel of the rabbi's doorway. His penetrating eyes set below a broad, shining forehead gazed submissively, expectant of the rabbi's words; ever since the rabbi's advent to Yerushalayim, he had become accustomed to receive such summonses.

He was aware that when he appeared before the *rav*, all of his knowledge and expertise in preparation of medicines and prescriptions were as naught. Here he must only listen and obey.

Who was this Reb Moshe, for whom the Brisker Gaon would delay the *shofar* blasts on *Rosh Hashanah* until he had completed his medical rounds?

The Brisker Rav's Personal Physician

Reb Moshe Jules was the son of a distinguished family in Hungary, all of whose sons had gained prominence through their capabilities. The family was also noted for its trustworthiness and honesty, and many valuable securities were entrusted in its hands.

The family pinned great hopes on young Moshe. All of his teachers predicted that he would fill one of the coveted rabbinical positions of Hungary. But young Moshe thought otherwise. From childhood on he yearned to go to Eretz Yisrael. As soon as the opportunity presented itself to him, he executed his hidden wish, emigrating to Yerushalayim-between-the-walls when he was only sixteen years old.

Upon his arrival he found that Yerushalayim did not lack people of spiritual prowess. The one thing the city did lack was a doctor. Our Sages valued the function of doctor so highly— Moshe used to think to himself—that they even went as far as forbidding residence in a city that did not harbor one. It struck him that the Holy City lacked precisely such a man, whose presence was all the more vital for Yerushalayim's rejuvenated settlement, since the city was built on desolate wasteland where disease and epidemic ran rampant. This matter caused many to forsake their principles and turn to the mission doctors who readily took advantage of their position.

Yerushalayim leaders did launch a full force battle against the mission's medical front, but with no alternative to that service, the fight proved difficult sevenfold.

Reb Moshe felt that he was the person capable of donating his efforts in this direction, and with the support and encouragement of the Torah leadership, took this yoke upon himself.

Thanks to his many talents, he had acquired in his youth a facility in many languages. He now began to study different medical volumes, tried his strength at diagnosing various illnesses and tested his capable hands at the preparation of medicines and herb mixtures. His marvelous intuition stood him in good stead and his concoctions succeeded. Slowly he earned a reputation as an expert physician. It was this proximity which enabled him to disclose at the funeral of the *gaon* in 5659, many awe-inspiring facts of the great man's behavior which were hidden from his very closest disciples.

He told, for example, that upon the frequent occasions when he was summoned to treat the great man's hernia which needed constant attention and from which he suffered greatly in his latter years, the *rav* would refuse to lower his hands below his waist—as a sign of purity which our Sages had testified to the credit of Rabbi Yehuda Hanassi—even though his pains were thus greatly increased and extended. The same was true when the *gaon* once summoned Reb Moshe for an intense pain which attacked him in his thighs. Reb Moshe wanted to examine his holy body, but the *gaon* refused to raise his hands above his head fearing the *Zohar's* admonition against it.

The Brisker Rav's trust in Reb Moshe did not lie in the

55

latter's medical know-how. Rather, he believed that Reb Moshe's very hands were endowed with miraculous, Heaven-sent powers to heal the sick, and that Reb Moshe the Tzaddik, as he would call him, had an astounding measure of Heavenly guidance in healing, even by virtue of his very appearance at the home of the patient. As accepted a medical authority as Reb Moshe was in Yerushalayim, it was the Brisker Rav who actually made him the unofficial physician of the city.

Whenever Reb Moshe came to treat a woman, he would customarily lower his large *yarmulke* until almost below his eyes for fear of evil thoughts. The *rav* noted this habit and fearing that it might interfere with his diagnoses, summoned the doctor to him.

"I promise you, my dear Reb Moshe," he said, "that as long as you fulfill your obligations wholeheartedly, you will forever be spared from evil thoughts concerning women."

Reb Moshe held on to many of the notes he received written in the *gaon's* own handwriting, expressing various requests. Three such notes were found among his possessions when he passed away.

The first note read, "Please give Reb Zelig to drink from my spice preparation, and may it do him good." Reb Zelig Braverman was one of the pure minded souls in the city who labored all his years in Torah and *mitzvos*. Aside from his total dedication to these in general, he sacrificed himself for one *mitzvah* in particular. Every Thursday he would close the *Gemara* from which he did not budge day or night, throw a knapsack over his back and make the rounds from house to house gathering donations of *challos*, fish and other *Shabbos* delicacies from Yerushalayim's good Jews. On Friday *erev Shabbos*, a long procession of poor people would line up outside his rickety

56

house where Reb Zelig would dispense the bounty from his sacks with a generous hand.

At one point, Reb Zelig began ailing in his legs and could no longer make the rounds. The poor people continued to request their weekly portions and Reb Zelig, in his dilemma, turned to the Brisker Rav for help. The *rav* gave him the above note for Reb Moshe.

This "spice drink" which Reb Moshe would dispense to many sick people, for all manner of ailments and conditions had a composition unknown to any Yerushalmi. Rumor had it that even gentile doctors who marveled at the efficacy of this potion tried to duplicate it or analyze its ingredients but never succeeded. The Brisker Rav's closer *talmidim* knew that Reb Moshe Jules simply gathered the spices upon which the *rav* recited the *havdalah* blessing after *Shabbos* and cooked them up in a strong wine, and behold, the miraculous potion.

The second note contained the following message. "Forgive me for bothering you but please be so good as to bandage Reb Michel's leg for three days."

What was wrong with this Reb Michel, pillar of the *halachic* authorities of the city, whom even Yerushalayim's own rabbi, Rav Shmuel Salant, would consult on questions of permission or prohibition? Reb Michel was the authority upon whose shoulders rested the responsibility for the city slaughterhouse. He was a noted expert on the special slaughter knives and their sharpening and an authority of the *kashrus* of lungs. Upon one occasion when Reb Michel took a knife from the *shochet* for inspection before the slaughter, the intended bull-victim suddenly broke away from his ropes and injured the inspector's foot, necessitating his absence from the slaughterhouse for some time. When the news of Reb Michel's absence circulated, some Yerushalayim Jews refused to eat meat altogether. The Brisker Rav learned of this abstention and sent the above note to Reb Moshe Jules, asking him to treat Reb Michel's leg for three days. Reb Moshe did as bid and within that week Reb Michel was able to return to his supervision at the slaughter-house, just in time for the city's residents to enjoy meat for *Shabbos.*

The third note read, "Please, Reb Moshe, be so good as to lay your hands over the eyes of young Shmuel Tefilinski."

Reb Shmuel Tefilinski, son of Reb Nesanel the Yerushalayim scribe, was known as an ascetic and saint throughout his life, preserving his eyes from all forbidden sights. Even in his later years, when the Eitz Chaim yeshivah moved its quarters from the Churva Synagogue in the Old City to the new building in the Machane Yehuda section of the new city, he would leave his house in Batei Broide and take the long roundabout road back and forth each day instead of going directly through the Machane Yehuda marketplace. He did so to avoid the women frequenting the market stalls.

Before his death Reb Shmuel sighed, "I will most assuredly not receive any reward for my vigilance over my eyes, since it is a trait so deeply ingrained in my blood." The truth is, however, that Reb Shmuel acquired this characteristic through great self sacrifice in his childhood, when he used to go through the city streets with one hand covering his eyes, as if he were reciting *Shema.* This habit affected his eyes until he began to suffer extensively. His father, Reb Nesanel, went to the Brisker Rav for advice and the above note to Reb Moshe was the result. Young Shmuel was cured of his pain by the medic's ministra-tion.

How had Reb Moshe gained such stature in the eyes of the

Brisker Rav that that mighty giant of Torah and piety should refer to him as "Reb Moshe the *Tzaddik*"? Yerushalayim Jews had various theories and speculations, but according to the wise *rebbetzin*, all these stories were merely idle chatter. She herself would tell the story as it had really happened.

The Gaon of Brisk ate the barest minimum at each meal. A year after the *rav's aliyah* to Yerushalayim, his pure body weakened and his wife who was so dedicated in her careful attention to his health, began cooking an extra portion of chicken in addition to the meal itself. But she did not gain anything thereby. The Gaon of Brisk would eat his chicken soup which was served as the first course and would thereafter refuse to touch both chicken and the main dish.

When the *rebbetzin* once came across the Yerushalayim physician, Reb Moshe Jules, she poured out her problem to him. "Why must you begin the meal with the customary soup?" he suggested. "Deviate from tradition by serving the *rav* his portion of chicken first. Let him eat that instead and fortify himself."

"*Oy, oy!*" the *rebbetzin* sighed. "Such a simple thing did not even enter my mind! It was not in vain that our Sages ruled that women's wisdom lies in the spindle alone. I did not even possess common sense in regard to simple dietary matters!"

On the following day at suppertime—the only meal that the *gaon* would eat during the day—the *rebbetzin* served her husband his main course first. The Gaon of Brisk took up the chicken bone and noticed that it was crooked. He inspected it.

"Apparently there was a break here that healed," the *gaon* said. "It may be *halachically* permissible, but I have never eaten meat which was at all questionable. Why must I be lenient now that I am old?"

59

The *gaon* now wished to know why the *rebbetzin* had changed the customary order of the meal, but fearing her distress, left it for the morrow when she volunteered the episode with the doctor, Reb Moshe Jules.

"If Reb Moshe had the good fortune of saving a Jew from questionable food, he must surely be a *tzaddik*," the great man asserted upon hearing the story. And from that time on, the leader of the Diaspora began calling the Yerushalayim doctor, "Reb Moshe the *Tzaddik*."

The Gaon of Brisk did not taste anything else from that meal for fear that it had touched the chicken or had been sprayed by the soup. Incidentally, from that incident onwards, some people of Yerushalayim tend to eat the main course first and the soup last for fear lest some question arise concerning the fowl, which they would thus discern before being contaminated by the soup.

Reb Moshe Jules now stood before the Brisker Rav, ready to lend a hand in curing Reb Efraim Nachman. The *gaon* told him to take a raw egg, half a cup of milk and a spoonful of honey and mix these together well, heat them and dispense the concoction to Reb Efraim Nachman.

Reb Efraim Nachman smiled bitterly. He wanted to explain to the *rav* that if the tens-of-potions of costly medicines which he had already ingested had not availed, surely this old fashioned grandmother's mixture would not help, but he was afraid to open his mouth. The *gaon* felt his hesitation and noted his nervous gestures. He knew what was pressing on the sick man's heart.

"Don't worry, Reb Efraim Nachman," the *rav* reassured him. "Reb Moshe Jules has special Providence guiding him. The Angel Rafael himself walks by his side!"

The sick man heard the rabbi's words and almost fainted.

Such explicit pronouncement from the greatest man of the generation upon whose every breath Diaspora Jewry hung trembling! Whose every word was carefully weighed and tested! He was now assured of his recovery.

The Gaon of Brisk continued. "Our Sages said that sometimes a man must be cured by one particular physician or by one specific drug. Was that not what I told you—that you came to Yerushalayim at the opportune time?"

Reb Efraim Nachman coughed his last cough and drank down the mixture. The *gaon* wished him a speedy and complete recovery, and he never coughed again until his death.

Reb Efraim Nachman remained in Yerushalayim for another two weeks. He knew that he owed his life to the Brisker Rav and before his departure he entrusted to him a considerable sum for the establishment of the orphanage besides an additional sum for the *gaon* to distribute as he saw fit among Yerushalayim Torah scholars. He took his leave, promising that he would be beholden to the *rav* for the rest of his days.

Rav Schlesinger's Warning

On the last day of his stay, Reb Efraim Nachman went to say goodbye to his good friend, Rav Akiva Yosef Schlesinger. Aside from the Gaon of Brisk and Reb Moshe Jules, no one in Yerushalayim knew of his sudden visit or the reason behind it, but Reb Efraim Nachman saw it his duty to tell Rav Akiva Yosef everything.

Rav Akiva Yosef heard about the *gaon's* medicine and began clapping his hands in wonder. "Ah, ah, how great that man is! How fortunate I am to know such a great person from

61

close, to have seen him in action!"

What did Rav Akiva Yosef actually mean by that? In 5645, five years after the foundation of the settlement of Petach Tikvah by devout Yerushalayim Jews under the impetus of Rav Akiva Yosef (actually the Gaon of Brisk served as president of the organization, the deed was on his name, the charter incorporated his ideas and the settlers signed a document accepting him as their supreme authority), the executive directors of the organization met at one of its thrice-yearly meetings to review the state of affairs and examine the efficacy of its rules. More than once members had been admonished or actually ousted from the group for nonconformity. This time, three cases of apparently severe infringements were brought up for discussion even though they entailed no actual violation of religious law.

The first case concerned member Z., father of a large family, who was being brought to task for withdrawing his sixteen-year-old son from *yeshivah* twice a week for two hours on a steady basis so that the youth could help him out in the fields. The charter read: "We are forbidden to remove our sons from Torah study to help us in the work at home or in the fields for any steady period before they reach the age of eighteen."

The second case concerned member D., who had been standing in his sheep pen an hour and a half before *Shabbos*, straining the milk. He had been warned several times but had ignored these admonitions. The charter stated: "A high banner shall be raised upon a lofty place to be visible throughout the borders of our settlement every *erev Shabbos* and *yom tov* afternoon. The *shofar* will also be sounded as a clear sign that all field work is to cease. Whoever tarries more than two hours beyond the raising of the banner and shall do so three times, will be duly punished."

(This amendment was adopted in Petach Tikvah by Rav Akiva Yosef and later instituted in Yerushalayim as well. He would, in fact, put his head out of his window which overlooked the *Kosel Hamaaravi* every Friday afternoon before candle-lighting time and give three blasts of the *shofar* as our Sages suggested.)

The third case concerned member L., who had required a worker for his chicken coop. He had contracted a worker who had been employed by his neighbor by offering him a higher wage. The Arab laborer had transferred to his employ. The charter read: "No man has the right to take a laborer, whether Jewish or gentile, who has already begun working for another as long as that other employer still requires his services, except if that person owed his laborer several days' wages and keeps putting him off. The worker, however, has the right to work for whomever he wishes."

One faction of the directors was for banishing these violators from the society while the majority, including Rav Akiva Yosef, which feared the total dissolution of the group, voted to allow them to remain on trial after a stringent warning.

The difference of opinions was presented to the Gaon of Brisk who ruled that according to law the violators should be ejected immediately. Rav Akiva Yosef had been surprised at this decision. Aside from the battles against elements threatening the purity of Torah education in which the Gaon of Brisk fought to the bitter end, he was known for his lenient ruling. Why had he come out so forcefully in this ruling?

The year 5649 arrived, a *shemitah* year. This was the first actual test for the renewed settlement in Eretz Yisrael which now owned vineyards and fields. The test of forsaking the toil of one's hands over the years was a most difficult one. It meant abandoning fields to man and beast, not sowing or plowing throughout an entire year as the Torah had directed. The majority of Petach Tikvah settlers withstood the test, but there were some who attempted to find loopholes to permit them to work in the fields.

The devout among Yerushalayim's population who heard of this conflict wondered how "foreign plantings" had found their way among the Torah true settlers of Petach Tikvah. The Gaon of Brisk, however, knew who stood behind them.

Michel Pines, one of the *Maskilim* sent by a well known organization in London which "concerned" itself with the education of Yerushalayim children, tried his hand at establishing a school for foreign languages and other secular subjects in Yerushalayim. Most Yerushalayim Jews did not penetrate to the man's true nature, since he was a learned man with all the religious trappings. It was the Gaon of Brisk who revealed Pines' true colors and thwarted his path until he was forced to leave the city. Pines managed somehow to purchase a home in Petach Tikvah and when the *shemitah* year came, he set out to wreak his revenge. He knew that the Gaon of Brisk, his sworn enemy, stood at the head of the fighters against leniency in the sabbatical prohibitions. He carefully investigated which of the settlers had in the past already dared to transgress the ordinances of the charter outlined by the *gaon* and made special efforts to befriend these people.

Chanukah arrived. The settlers of Petach Tikvah filled the *beis midrash*, leaning over their *Gemaros*. Pines' group, however, went out to plow their fields, the initial plowing after the first rains.

When the Gaon of Brisk learned of this, he dropped all connection with Petach Tikvah and resigned from his post.

64

Petach Tikvah became an ugly morass and the religious settlement began declining. Rav Akiva Yosef saw all his labor in establishing that agricultural settlement going down the drain and wept, "Alas, the Gaon of Brisk foresaw all this long ago."

Rav Akiva Yosef now reviewed this entire chapter before his friend Reb Efraim Nachman and repeated, "Did I not tell you that I saw the Gaon of Brisk in action?

"Perhaps," he continued, "we were at fault when we showered the settlers of Petach Tikvah with all the benefits in the world. We spoiled them. The trial of wealth is a great one, indeed, being immeasurably greater than the tests of poverty and want. Only isolated cases succeed in escaping the pitfalls of wealth as our Torah warned us, 'And Yerushalayim grew fat and rebelled.'"

Rav Akiva Yosef became excited. "Only this week," he continued, "I touched on this subject in the book I am about to publish, *Toras Yechiel*, in explaining the verses, 'And Avraham was very heavy in cattle, silver and gold. And he continued his journeys.' Even though Avraham was vastly wealthy, he continued to journey along the identical path, the path of G-d, as before. This was not so with Lot of whom the Torah says, 'And Lot who went with Avraham also owned sheep and cattle.' And further on, 'And Lot travelled from the east.' Rashi comments that he removed himself from G-d (playing on the dual meaning of the word '*kedem*', east, and before, referring to the One Who was before this world). So you see, not everyone can withstand this trial."

Rav Akiva Yosef stretched his hand out to Reb Efraim Nachman, wishing him again good health, and they parted. On the morrow Reb Efraim Nachman left for Jaffa, and within that week boarded the ship that was to take him back to Canada.

Seated in his luxurious, spacious, first-class cabin, Reb Efraim Nachman had a chance to examine what had happened to him in the last period, beginning with a half year previously when he had begun consulting the top specialists who had not given him more than a few weeks to live. He recalled his resolution to go to Yerushalayim to beg for his life from the Cedars of Lebanon—the Gaon of Brisk and his friends. Now he was returning, healthy and whole, to his home and family.

He recalled his strange leavetaking with Rav Akiva Yosef Schlesinger and the latter's emotional pronouncement about the trial of wealth.

"Have I not visited Yerushalayim many times?" Reb Efraim Nachman wondered to himself. "Have I not said good-bye to Rav Akiva Yosef on previous occasions? Why did he never mention such thoughts to me before? Does this *tzaddik* think that I have G-d-forbid veered from the right path, that I have become less observant in *mitzvah* performance than before?"

Tears gathered in the corners of his eyes and he murmured a short prayer to Hashem asking Him to grant him life and preserve him from error. For had not our Sages warned, "Let a man not believe in himself until the day of death!"

The mild Mediterranean air, the calm sea waves and the gentle rocking of the ship in the caressing breeze quieted his tumultuous thoughts. After about ten weeks of travelling, the ship docked at Canadian shores.

Spiritual Decline

Reb Efraim Nachman returned home completely cured to the joy of his family and many friends. He returned to his business, his *shiurim* and his charitable practices. For the next nine years he knew no sickness whatsoever. One night, two weeks after the bitter news of the Gaon of Brisk's demise shook the Jewish exile, Reb Efraim Nachman returned home after *davening maariv* shaken and weak. It was 5659, and the day was *Tu B'shvat*. His family and friends who had gathered that evening to taste fruits from Eretz Yisrael in honor of *Tu Bishvat* were taken aback at his pale appearance. Before he had a chance to taste the *esrog* comfiture brought especially by a messenger from Yerushalayim, he fainted. The doctor who was speedily summoned found him on the verge of death. There were several *minyanim* of people present at the time and in their presence he recited the *Shema* with a mighty effort and passed away.

Reb Efraim Nachman had a son, Yechezkel. During his father's lifetime he maintained all of that devout, G-d-fearing person's religious practices, performing difficult *mitzvos* along with the simpler ones. He tithed his profits to the poor and to Torah scholars, maintained regular study periods in the *beis midrash*, but most important of all, kept his father's practice of sending huge sums of money to the Torah institutions and scholars in the Holy City. Yechezkel kept up this way of life for several years after his father's death as well.

At a young age, Yechezkel married a girl from a wealthy family who bore him two sons and two daughters. His father-in-law presented him with a huge fortune which increased his material wealth stupendously.

The Reform Movement was then on the march in America and Canada. Men of weak character from the ranks of American Jewry began to adapt their life style to their gentile neighbors. Theaters were the popular form of entertainment. Plays promoted by charitable organizations as a ready form of income took on increasingly commercial tones. And the wives of wealthy Jewish businessmen, who were mainly liberated from household duties by their hired maids and servants, could not withstand the lure.

At first, Yechezkel Radiner maintained firm vigil over his household refusing to allow its members to visit these places of iniquity. It once happened, however, that an institution with the trappings of orthodoxy sponsored and opera titled, *The Sale of Joseph*, publicizing in huge letters on all posters that "proceeds would go to charitable organizations." Yechezkel's wife and daughters succeeded in convincing him that no harm would come from attending. On the night of the performance, the society matron and her two daughters wore their fanciest clothes, bedecked themselves with clusters of jewelry and hurried to arrive at the theater at the appointed time.

From that time on, they always found some excuse for attending any desired performance. At first they attempted to find the religious angle to any given play. Before *Chanukah*, for example, it was surely worthwhile to see a play called *Judith*, while it became a veritable *mitzvah* to view a *Queen Esther* performance at *Purim* time. Bit by bit they were drawn to the more lurid plays. Yechezkel made peace with this, too. Did not the wives and daughters of his associates also behave thus throughout greater America? Should he stand out by being the only fanatic? Did the matter in any way affect his own *shiurim*, prayers or his charitable efforts?

The morality of Yechezkel Radiner's house slowly deteriorated. His wife and daughters began adapting their dress to the apparel of their more liberal friends. Depraved newspapers and magazines soon penetrated into their home, at first just to keep them posted on the latest plays, but later for their own sake.

Kashrus observance was neglected. Yechezkel himself, who grew accustomed quickly enough to the new trend in his home, hardly felt himself deteriorating only a step behind his wife and daughters.

The pre-*Yom Tov* season arrived, and Yechezkel's sons, who returned home for their vacation, began joining their mother and sisters in their theater excursions. When the two boys returned late after their first visit to the stage and vividly described what they had seen that evening, Yechezkel complimented their cunning perception of the event, unaware of his own reluctant approval. The younger son now reminded his father that with *Pesach* just around the corner, he intended to steal the *afikoman*. He expected as his reward, he announced, a movie camera, so that he, too, could capture life as he had seen it on the stage. And Yechezkel promised to honor his request.

One evening during *Chol Hamoed Pesach*, a resplendent carriage arrived to take Yechezkel, his wife and their four children to the theater to see a satirical show entitled, *The Jerusalem Jews of the Monthly Stipend*. Yechezkel returned from the theater a different man. He forgot all about his tithing, his charity, his study periods and his prayers. This trend progressed with the speed of a runaway cart. His sons were removed from *yeshivah* and enrolled in the university so that they would "amount to something." The wig which had covered his wife's head for the past two years, replacing the kerchief she had formerly worn, was also removed and she now began to bare her head in order to resemble other American women, both Jewish and non-Jewish.

Yechezkel was too embarrassed to appear in the same *shul* where he had always *davened*. He transferred over to a Reform temple.

69

Since the temple was far form the religious neighborhood where he lived, Yechezkel had to make the long trip on *Shabbos* by foot until he finally decided to do what the Reform rabbi himself did. Every *Shabbos*, after he had joined his family in a rich meal, he entered a fine coach, especially ordered for that hour. With silver-collared *tallis* under his arm, he drove to the temple. Yechezkel Radiner became a full-fledged *Shabbos* defiler. The years passed and he forgot his entire past, his father's home and his origins.

The Transformation Wrought by a Little Letter

5674 came and with it the First World War. As with all wars fought between nations, the Jews bore a heavy toll of the suffering, and foremost among these were the Jews of Yerushalayim whose very lives depended upon outside income.

Hunger reigned supreme. Communally alert citizens of Yerushalayim energetically established a central kitchen called "The House of Bread and Tea." This group of active settlers was headed by Reb Shlomo Roth and Reb Zanvil Spitzer, two of the trustees of Kolel Shomrei Hachomos; Reb Yonasan Binyamin Horowitz, the Frankfurter Rabbi; Reb Naftali Parush; Reb Zev Mintzburg and Reb Yerucham Fishel, all from the boards of various *kolelim*.

The will to act and accomplish something for the cause was great, but from where were they to derive support to maintain such a communal kitchen? The directors began to rummage among old receipt books of the various organizations in the hope of renewing ties with former philanthropists in the Diaspora that had dissolved. Suddenly they came across the name of the

70

great giver, Reb Yechezkel Radiner from Toronto, son of the famous philanthropist Reb Efraim Nachman.

"Whatever happened?" Reb Yonasan Binyamin turned to Reb Shlomo Roth. "It has been years since this Reb Yechezkel, who continued his father's great work for many years, has donated as much as a penny to Yerushalayim institutions!"

"He must have died young," Reb Shlomo replied.

"Anything is possible," Reb Yonasan Binyamin replied, "but we are at fault for not having handled matters efficiently. Why did we have to wait until the last minute, until we began drowning in our troubles?"

The two sat right down and composed a beautiful letter, written in the fine, curlicued script of Reb Yonasan Binyamin's hand, in which they described the gloomy circumstances of the Holy City and its inhabitants and especially the dire state of its Torah scholars.

> To the honorable, rabbinic, philanthropic, Reb Yechezkel, *shilta*, son of our dear friend, the munificent, gracious, true supporter of Yerushalayim and its wise men, Reb Efraim Nachman Radiner of blessed memory . . ."

Knowing the close friendship Reb Efraim Nachman had enjoyed with Rav Akiva Yosef Schlesinger, they went down to the latter's house to have him sign the letter as well. At first the two were amazed that Rav Akiva Yosef refused to put his signature on the paper. It was only after much intensive pleading and after the deleting of most of the flowery descriptions regarding Yechezkel's famous generosity, that he finally agreed. That very day, Reb Shlomo Roth travelled to Beirut, where he found, in return for a round sum of money, a gentile traveller willing to deliver the letter to its address. The postal system in Eretz Yisrael had completely broken down.

Yechezkel Radiner received the letter on *Shabbos* morning. He was accustomed to open his mail on *Shabbos*, but seeing the address on the envelope and the names of the senders, he was thoroughly shaken. His hands seemed to turn to stone. He hid the letter away to be opened later, right after *Shabbos*, but throughout the day he was uneasy, fitful. His thoughts careened about inside his head as if he were drunk. Yechezkel's wife and children sensed the sudden change from his face and tried to extract some information about the origin of his consternation, but he remained silent. His children suggested that a doctor be summoned, but he refused to hear of it.

The doctor did appear, on *Motzei Shabbos*, summoned by Yechezkel's wife, at precisely the moment he had been prepared to open the letter. The doctor examined him thoroughly from head to toe and diagnosed that he was as healthy as an ox. He was merely suffering from depression. Yechezkel merely laughed at him. Meanwhile he dispatched his older son to several business associates with whom he had planned to confer that evening, postponing the meeting to later on that week.

He now was free to open the letter. Taking it with him into his private office, he locked the door behind him and opened it with a twinge of trepidation and began reading, "To the honorable, rabbinical . . ." A stream of tears cascaded down his cheeks. Feelings of remorse welled up in him, and he begged Hashem, to Whom he had sinned so grievously, to take his life. He read another line of the letter which had meanwhile become sodden with tears. His eyes continued to stream. He wailed and bawled like a newborn infant. "How often did my father mention these people whose names are signed below, these pure minded saints of Jerusalem who do not know the true reason for my having ceased my donations."

Hearing his moaning, Yechezkel's wife and children tried to peek through the keyhole. The youngest son who had been added to the family five years before, gave a toss of his long hair, as his mother had taught him to do and commented, "Father has grown old. He is senile."

"Yes," the mother concurred. "Even the doctor said that if he shows no improvement, we will be forced to institutionalize him in a mental hospital. Difficult times are upon us, children." She then turned her attention to her personal grooming in order not to arrive late at the play scheduled for that evening. The carriage had already been summoned and it soon devoured wife and children and was swallowed up itself by the bustling Saturday evening crowds.

Yechezkel was aware of what was happening behind the door and heaved a sigh. "Ai, ai, this is my faithful wife! This modern, intelligent American woman! She has already relegated her husband to a mental hospital while she rushes to her theatrical performance. And my children . . ." Yechezkel tried to recall the words of the prophet, "Sons have I reared . . . and they . . ." but here his memory betrayed him. "Let me see, did I not tear open the envelope before *davening Maariv*? Before making *havdalah* over wine?"

Yechezkel put on his hat and jacket, rummaged around in his drawers until he found a *siddur* and stood in a corner of the room. In a tear-choked voice he *davened Maariv*, after a silence of fifteen years during which he had not spoken a single word to his Maker. He now intoned, "You have graced us with the study of Your Torah and have taught us to perform Your laws . . . Our Father, Our King, commence for us the coming days in peace, free of all sin, cleansed of all iniquity, adhering to Your fear . . ."

He maintained his emotional equilibrium with difficulty and continued, "Return us, O Father, to Your Torah, draw us near, O our King, to Your service . . . Forgive us Father for . . . we have sinned . . . pardon us O King, for we have transgressed . . ." He finished the *shemoneh esrei* which had taken him two hours. "And all those who rise up and intend to harm me, speedily confound their plans and spoil their thoughts." He included his wife and children as well in this prayer. "No, I am not a candidate for a mental institution," concluded Yechezkel. The conversation he had overheard behind the door had actually strengthened his spirit, showing him to what depths one could plummet. "A Jew devoid of Torah and fear of G-d is a most cruel creature," he murmured to himself.

He left his apartment and went to a religious neighbor who lived in the same building, a neighbor whom he and his family had always mocked when they were in high spirits, and begged to borrow a cup of wine for *havdalah*. The neighbor was shocked but hurried to comply, whispering to his wife in passing, "Yechezkel did, after all, have a great father."

Yechezkel Radiner became a complete *baal teshuvah*.

The following days were serious ones in the Radiner household; arguments abounded. His wife and older children tried to influence him to take the doctor's prescriptions and to enter a hospital for a short period in order to recuperate from his melancholia. Yechezkel, in his turn, admonished them that they, too, should improve their ways and repent, for man had not been created for revelry. A Jew who lives the life of a gentile is worse than an animal, he argued. He urged them to abandon their wicked ways for which he perhaps was to blame, having followed their initiative instead of having restrained them. But his words fell on deaf ears. His household was thoroughly steeped in sin.

Slowly it began to dawn upon Yechezkel's family that they were not dealing with a case of insanity at all. Their father had simply become a complete *baal teshuvah*.

Yechezkel, who was a vastly wealthy man, now began neglecting his numerous business affairs to spend most of his day in the *beis knesses* or in the home of the rabbi of the city. During the next few months, he still tried to influence his wife and children to repent but seeing his efforts were futile, he began slowly selling his vast wealth and transferring the proceeds to the institutions of charity and Torah in the Holy City. The Jews of Yerushalayim began to breathe easy.

Toronto reverberated from the chapter of Yechezkel Radiner. The Reform community was struck a mighty blow by his repentance but despite the great wonder, the news that Yechezkel had decided to divorce his wife and emigrate to Yerushalayim hit the city like a thunderbolt.

Yechezkel's wife and children consulted a lawyer and after six weeks a property settlement was made over to them. In 5678, at the wane of the World War and four years after he had received that fateful letter, Yechezkel left the country forever and went to live in Eretz Yisrael.

None of the communal figures in Yerushalayim knew anything about this entire chapter in Yechezkel's life, but they would occasionally argue among themselves over who actually was at fault for having broken contact with him originally and whose credit it was for having resumed it.

From a Palace to a Hallway

Yechezkel arrived in Yerushalayim right before the High Holidays, and for the first time in his life his foot stepped on the consecrated earth. For the first few weeks he slept in the city's hostel for the poor, making no contact with anyone. Each day he would visit the *Kosel Hamaaravi* and pour out his heart before the One Who dwelled in that place, begging to be forgiven for his sins, and thanking Hashem for having enlightened his eyes before his death. But the main thrust of his prayers was that Hashem put similar wisdom in the heart of his family and assist them to return to their true origins.

On the eve of *Sukkos*, Yechezkel slept in the small *sukkah* adjoining the hostel. That night his father appeared to him, smiling. Yechezkel was taken aback. It was the first time in all the years since his father's death that he had dreamed of him. His father now bore the news that his repentance had been accepted. He begged him to make his presence known to the wise men of Yerushalayim, especially to his friend of yore, Rav Akiva Yosef Schlesinger. Yechezkel awoke. It was midnight. He hurried to the *Kosel* to thank Hashem for the encouraging tidings that his repentance had been accepted.

On the first day of *Chol Hamoed Sukkos*, Yechezkel donned his best clothes, as in former days, and went to visit Reb Yonasan Binyamin Horowitz to make his acquaintance. Reb Yonasan Binyamin greeted him joyously, embracing and kissing him. "You are the one who saved Yerushalayim during its most difficult period."

Yechezkel, who had meanwhile grown a beard and *peyos*, burst into bitter weeping. He then poured out his entire life's story, describing how the rabbi's letter had caused him to return

76

to the fold of his people. Reb Yonasan Binyamin was shaken to hear this almost unbelievable tale and sighed, "*Oy*, how severely we *askanim* will have to account for our deeds. Who knows the power of one little letter? How many countless lives can be saved by one such little letter!"

Yechezkel now begged the rabbi not to divulge his identity to anyone for he wished to remain unknown in Yerushalayim, living a life of modesty and simplicity. After transferring to Reb Yonasan Binyamin a bundle containing most of his money and property which he wished to dedicate to institutions of Torah and charity, he related his dream and asked in the name of his father's friendship that the rabbi help him fulfill the deceased man's wish-to make the acquaintance of Rav Akiva Yosef.

Reb Yonasan Binyamin promised to preserve his secret and agreed to take him to Rav Akiva Yosef on the Sunday of the holiday.

Rabbi Yosef the *Tzaddik*

En route with Reb Yonasan Binyamin to the home of Rav Akiva Yosef, Yechezkel's thoughts were in a turmoil. He was considering how to introduce himself to the *tzaddik* of whom his father, Reb Efraim Nachman, had spoken so much. Would he be able to withstand the experience? Might he not faint on the spot when he merely stepped over the threshold of the *tzaddik's* doorway? He recalled something similar in the Torah, when Yosef revealed his identity to his brothers. How ashamed the tribes of G-d had been to gaze upon Yosef's face, because of the one sin they had committed, even though they had had valid rationales behind their actions. And he, stained with guilt from

77

head to foot, a sinner and an instrument for the sins of his family, how would he reveal himself to this *tzaddik* Yosef?

He arrived at Rav Akiva Yosef's house while he was still wrapped up in thought. To his immense surprise, he saw the *tzaddik* himself emerging and coming forward with outstretched hand in welcome! "*Shalom aleichem*, Reb Yechezkel. Why are you so embarrassed? Did our Sages not teach us that 'the heights that *baalei teshuvah* reach cannot be attained by complete *tzaddikim*?'"

What has happened here? Reb Yonasan Binyamin wondered. How did Rav Akiva Yosef Schlesinger know who this stranger was?

But Rav Akiva Yosef told them immediately that on the eve of *Succos* he had been visited by Yechezkel's father in a dream. The latter had related all that had transpired with his son, including his emigration to Yerushalayim, and he had asked sincerely that he befriend him.

Rav Akiva Yosef now related that Reb Efraim Nachman had appeared to him previously, several years before when Yechezkel and his family were just beginning to lose their spiritual footing, to admit that only then did he understand the rabbi's warning about the trials of riches. In the first dream, he had asked the rabbi to pray for his son and the Radiner family and ask Hashem to infuse them with a spirit of purity from Heaven which would assist them to repent.

"And now you are here, Yechezkel," Rav Akiva Yosef concluded. "The day will yet come when your children will return to true Judaism and come here as well."

Yechezkel's eyes lit up. He wiped away tears of gladness with his handkerchief upon hearing the news which he had so longed for. He also understood from the *tzaddik's* words that his wife would not similarly repent. He was glad now that he had been wise enough to divorce her.

They all entered the large *sukkah* in the courtyard. Rav Akiva Yosef himself served his guests, all the while encouraging Yechezkel. "You have attained ultimate repentance, Yechezkel. You can now return to normal life and business here in Yerushalayim. But be sure you maintain regular periods of Torah study-this is one thing that your father observed with a high degree of self-sacrifice. I am certain that had you persevered in your study periods during the past, you would not have had to go through all that you did. You would not have lost your family in the process."

Rav Akiva Yosef interrupted his own steady stream of speech with the blessing for sitting in the *succah* which he recited upon a cup of wine, urging his guests to do likewise. Then he continued, "Yesterday, on *Shabbos*, we all read the verse in *Koheles*, 'If the ruling spirit rises in you, do not abandon your place.' Come, Yechezkel, let us open a *sefer* and see together how the *Targum* translates this."

The *tzaddik* opened up a *Koheles* and read, "If the evil inclination gains ascendancy over you, keep your hold over one particular worthy practice which you have and do not abandon it, for Torah was created as a remedy for the world, to help (people) abandon and erase great sins."

Yechezkel accepted upon himself all that Rav Akiva Yosef had said concerning Torah study, but he refused to consider resuming his former life of business enterprise. He had come to Yerushalayim with a firm resolve to seclude himself in obscurity, to live like one of the poor people and thus serve his G-d to Whom he had sinned, privately, without anyone knowing about his former status and wealth.

Convinced of his firm resolution, Rav Akiva Yosef did not attempt to interfere. On the contrary, he even helped him find a small room off a little corridor in one of the rows of three houses of Batei Ungarin. Here Yechezkel spend his last years, in Yerushalayim, alone and unknown. The residents of the neighborhood took to calling him "Yechezkel Bachur."

About two years before his death, Yechezkel had the good fortune to hear the news that he had hoped and prayed for so expectantly—of his children's return to their religious origins and the true way of life. Their mother had passed away suddenly.

The Radiner family had requested one of the *meshulachim* from a well known Yerusalayim institution, who was in Toronto at the time to collect funds for the Eitz Chaim *yeshivah*, to eulogize their mother in exchange for a substantial fee. The *meshulach* asked them about their father and having learned the truth, succeeded in influencing the entire family to repent. The children tried to discover where their father lived in Yerushalayim but did not succeed.

When the thirty-day mourning period for Yechezkel Bachur had elapsed and surviving *askanim* of the previous generation had uncovered the secret of his true identity, they informed the family in Canada. His sons and sons-in-law all came to Yerushalayim to pray upon his grave.

The promise of the *tzaddik*, Rav Akiva Yosef Schlesinger, had been realized to the full.

On the slope of the Prophet's section of the Mount of Olives cemetery there is a tombstone whose letters have become rubbed out with the years. But one can still make out the words, written in the same phrasing of the fateful letter that Reb Yonasan Binyamin Horowitz sent to Toronto, describing the difficult times that Yerushalayim was undergoing.

> Here Lies Buried
> The Magnificent Righteous *Rav*
> Who Gave Bountifully to the Poor
> Rabbi Yechezkel Radiner of Blessed Memory
> (Known here in Yerushalayim as Yechezkel Bachur)
> Died on the 15th of *Shvat* 5694

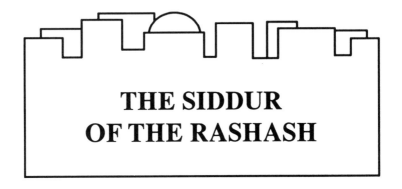

THE SIDDUR
OF THE RASHASH

The *Siddur* Vanishes Again

Rav Yaakov Leib Levi, *Rosh Av Beis Din* of the Holy City, was a man of most impressive appearance. He was built solidly and had a towering stature. His clothing was always well groomed and handsome; his light Yerushalayim caftan was never marred by a spot or wrinkle, as everyone knew.

He exuded a certain aura of charm and grace. He turned a pleasing expression to all, an inner joy overflowing into his face. His very stature was regal and when he passed through the streets of Yerushalayim, Rav Yaakov's appearance and beauty would attract glances even from non-Jews.

Arabs and Turkish policemen alike, making their rounds through the streets of the Old City, would gaze after him respectfully and make way for him as they huddled within winding alleyways to let him pass on his way to the *Kosel* or the *beis din* chambers.

That was only on the surface. Inside it was different; his heart mourned constantly. His entire being was like a broken earthenware vessel. He fasted often. All of his days were filled with suffering and with the trials of child-rearing.

All this, however, had no effect upon his brimming schedule of Torah study and prayer which he maintained with remarkable joy. At all times his eyes and heart were attuned to those oppressed by troubles or embittered by misfortune, to encourage them and improve their bitter lot.

The *rav* was a full-bodied and brave man, never knowing fear or trepidation. His son, Reb Mordechai, did see him, however, trembling and quaking twice in his lifetime, and then so severely that even those standing by, vibrated with him.

The first occasion was on *Rosh Chodesh Av* in 5637, when the Gaon of Brisk, Rav Yehoshua Leib Diskin arrived within the gates of Yerushalayim to settle. All the eminent personalities in the city went out to pay him homage, among them, Reb Yaakov Leib. At the moment that the Gaon of Brisk extended his hand to him in greeting, Rav Yaakov Leib began trembling, his knees shaking and his teeth chattering.

The second time was in 5638, when the Gaon of Brisk and his *beis din* proclaimed a ban on secular schools. When Rav Yaakov Leib dipped his pen in ink for the first signature, his appearance underwent a complete transformation, rendering him unrecognizable. His skin turned a pasty white and his bones shivered as if he had been seized by a violent fever.

Rav Yaakov Leib's second son, Reb Aharon, used to add that whenever he saw his father taking out the Rashash's *siddur* and holding it, his hands shook as if they had just touched burning coals.

One *Shabbos*, on the eleventh of *Elul*, Rav Yaakov sensed

that he was about to depart this world. He called his son Reb Yisrael to him and told him his last wishes, including instructions concerning the Rashash's *siddur*.

Towards *minchah* of that *Shabbos*, in the sacred hour of "*raava deraavin*," Rav Yaakov Leib's pure soul ascended to the *yeshivah shel maalah*.

After his death, the holy *siddur* again disappeared. And no one in the Holy City had any idea why this treasure, upon which all of the elite of Israel had their eyes affixed, had again been concealed.

Rav Yaakov had instructed his son Reb Yisrael concerning the hand-written *siddur*, but no one knew exactly what he had said. As for Reb Yisrael, he was taciturn by nature and no one could squeeze a word out of him. Even when his relatives and friends pressed him to reveal the whereabouts of the *siddur*, he would reply curtly, "Don't worry, it is in trusty hands."

A year passed. The fate of the *siddur* was unknown and the fact of its existence was almost entirely forgotten.

Three years after Rav Yaakov's death, his beloved son, Reb Yisrael, suddenly passed away. Yerushalayim was shaken by the sad news. Only then were *Yerushalmi's* reminded of the Rashash's *siddur* and its shuttling back and forth, but now they had no one to ask. They thought that Reb Yisrael had been the only one who knew the secret of its whereabouts but that he had taken that secret with him to his grave.

A Thanksgiving Celebration in the Home of Reb David'l

Among those who continuously investigated the whereabouts of the Rashash's *siddur*, there was one who stood out in his curiosity. This was Rabbi Naftali Hertz Halevi, Rabbi of Jaffa, whose achievements in *Kabbalah* equalled his strength in revealed Torah. He had heard much about the *siddur* but had never had the privilege of seeing it despite all his efforts to that end.

One time, during the Ten Days of Repentance of the year 5654, Rabbi Naftali was suddenly seized with a strong desire to find the *siddur*. He had been studying the *Yom Kippur* prayers when a difficulty in explanation had arisen. He was certain that the Rashash's *siddur* contained the answer to his quest.

The atmosphere of the impending *Yamim Noraim*, the Days of Awe which suffused his entire being, increased his longing to see the *siddur*. He could not sleep at night for longing. Besides, he had just completed his work of commentary on the *siddur* and this particular gap bothered him sorely.

Having no other choice, the Rabbi of Jaffa decided to go specially to Yerushalayim and try his luck there. Perhaps, with help from Heaven, he might find his heart's desire, the coveted *siddur*.

"*Davka* right now?" the *rebbetzin* asked him, "a few days before *Yom Kippur* when people are constantly coming with *halachic* questions? Now you want to leave the city? Can't you delay the trip until after all the holidays?"

"No, I cannot possibly postpone this trip," was his reply.

Hakadosh Baruch Hu sits on high and arranges matches down below. On the very day that Rabbi Naftali Hertz came to his decision to go to Yerushalayim and search for the *siddur*, he received two invitations from that city. One was delivered by the Brisker Gaon's personal messenger and the second, by mail, from his friend, Reb David'l Tzvi Shlomo Biderman of Lelov, son of Rav Elazar Mendel.

85

He had not the faintest idea why Rav Yehoshua Leib was asking him to come, nor could the messenger offer a conjecture for the urgent invitation. Reb David'l's invitation was explicit, however, requesting Rabbi Naftali to partake in a *seudas hoda'ah*, a feast of thanksgiving.

By the following evening, the Rabbi of Jaffa was in Yerushalayim. Asking himself where to go first, he decided to give preference to the *mitzvah* at hand, the thanksgiving celebration, and only afterwards to go to Rav Yehoshua Leib.

What was the cause for celebration?

Upon one of the slopes adjacent to the Spring of Shiloach, in the village of Silwan, there lived an Armenian Catholic named Treifus. This coarse, uncouth man was an animal trader and a rabid anti-semite besides.

One Friday, this gentile's nineteen-year-old son was passing by the Nissen Beck synagogue just as the steps were being washed. He slipped and fell, dying instantly from cerebral hemorrhage.

The entire city shook with the news. The evil Treifus took advantage of his son's death to feed his desire for revenge against the Jerusalem populace by informing the authorities that his son had been willfully murdered. Later, when he brought his son to burial, he swore before a huge crowd of Arabs that he would avenge his only son's blood at the first opportunity.

Some days later, the Admor Reb David'l Biderman left his home as was his usual custom, to immerse himself in the *mikvah* of the Silwan village which is said to be the *mikvah* of Rabbi Yishmael Kohein Gadol. Treifus noticed the lone figure and his anger seethed within him. Here, at last, was his chance to revenge himself against the Jews. He climbed up to the roof of his home and threw a heavy iron bar on top of the *tzaddik's* head.

The latter escaped death by a hair-breadth. As a sign of gratitude for the miracle he had experienced, Reb David'l was now tendering a *mitzvah* feast for all the great men of the Holy City.

The cream of Yerushalayim Torah society accepted the invitation, *chassidim* and *Perushim*, Sefardics and Ashkenazis. Standing out among the guests were, Reb Shneur Zalman of Lublin, author of *Toras Chesed*; Rav Yosef Chaim Sonnenfeld; Rav Akiva Yosef Schlesinger, author of *Lev Haivri*; Rav Tzvi Michel Shapiro, author of *Tzitz Hakadosh*; Rav Eliezer Dan Ralbag; Rav Zevulan Charlap; Rabbi Naftali Hertz Halevi from Jaffa; Rabbi Beinish Salant; Rabbi Eliezer Lipa Berlin, brother of the Netziv; Rabbi Shlomo Zalman Porush; Rabbi Shalom Leib Eisenbach, author of *Be'er Yitzchak*; Rabbi Alexander Ziskind-Shachor; Rabbi Avraham Abeli; Rabbi Binyamin Stemper; Rabbi Tzvi Aryeh Mezhirecher; Reb Yom Tom Yedid Halevi; the *kabbalist* Rav Chaim Shaul Dvik Hacohen; Rabbi Avraham Chaim Pinso; Rav Yeshaya and his son, Rav Yaakov Orenstein and many more.

During the meal, Reb David'l was asked by his guests to recount the praises of Hashem.

"Our Sages tell that Rav Sheishes, who was blind, once accompanied a group going to the king," he said. "He met a Tzedoki on the way who asked him this question.

"'Please explain something. Whole vessels are necessary to draw water from the river, but who needs broken vessels by the river? You cannot see—why then were you brought here?'

"'Even though the light of my eyes has been extinguished, nevertheless, I see better than you!'

"Just then a Roman division from the king's escort passed making considerable noise. 'Here comes the king!' the Tzedoki commented to Rav Sheishes.

"'No, you are mistaken,' Rav Sheishes replied. 'The king has not yet arrived.'

"After a while another unit of royal guard passed by, again raising a din. 'Here comes the king!' the Tzedoki cried out again, but Rav Sheishes contradicted him, 'That is not the king.'

"When the third train advanced, this time in silence, Rav Sheishes pointed his finger, 'The king is passing by now,' and recited the blessing one says when seeing royalty, 'Who has bestowed of His glory upon flesh and blood.'

"Our Sages ask what eventually happened to that Tzedoki. Some say that his eyes were gouged out, others say that Rav Sheishes looked in his direction and transformed him into a heap of bones.

"When I was a boy," Reb David'l reflected, "I always wondered about that question. Were it not for our Sages' question, no one would think that something had to happen to the Tzedoki!

"It appears, however, that *chazal* were convinced that if someone slighted a sage like Rav Sheishes, he must necessarily be punished. Hashem does not overlook or forgive the pain of His dear sons. That is why the *Gemara* asks about the Tzedoki's punishment.

"I was reminded of this story this week when I heard about the death of Treifus' son. I recall in my childhood seeing that very Treifus, who was then but a lad, sitting on a bench on Yehudim Street. A blind, elderly Jew once passed by and Treifus stuck his foot out to trip him. The old man fell and hurt his head, much blood spurting from the wound. I think that he was one of the *nistarim* of the Old City.

"Behold, assembled friends and rabbis, how *Hakadosh Baruch Hu* avenged the shame and blood of that old man, by visiting Triefus' son with a similar punishment, measure by measure."

As soon as the Sefardic Sage, Reb Yom Tov Yedid Halevi, heard Reb David'l waxing enthusiastic about *tzaddikim* and the matter of reward and retribution, he waited for him to finish and then added his own few words.

"A similar story happened to Rav Shalom Sharabi, the Rashash, the head of the *mekubalim* here in the Old City when he still lived in Damascus, his greatness concealed from the public," he related. "The wealthy businessman, Reb Shaul Parchi, hired young Shalom as his wagoner. It happened once that Rav Shalom was so involved in his deep otherworldly thoughts that he let the reins slip from his hands. The horses ran rampant until the coach finally came to a halt.

"Pressed by the urgency of his business, Reb Shaul was incensed at the delay and slapped his driver on the cheek. This act was considered an unintentional one since Reb Shaul did not know the real worth of his wagoner, but that night a tremendous fire raged in Reb Shaul's mansion. His entire fortune was wiped out and he and his sons became beggars overnight."

While Reb Yom Tov stood telling this story about the Rashash, Rav Yosef Chaim Sonnenfeld glanced at Rabbi Naftali Hertz and noticed tears rolling down his cheeks.

In reply to his inquiry as to the cause of tears at this time of rejoicing, Rabbi Naftali Hertz replied that the very mention of the Rashash's name re-aroused a longing and desire for the Rashash's *siddur* which had disappeared. This was, after all, the reason for his coming to Yerushalayim.

"You may be comforted," Rav Yosef Chaim turned to him, "for in our midst is a man who is capable of transcribing the *siddur* entirely from memory after its having stayed by him just one night. He is none other than the great author of *Toras Chesed*."

Rabbi Naftali refused to be consoled. He wished desperately to see the sacred *siddur* with his own eyes.

"I am certain that with the help of Hashem, you will yet behold the *siddur* today," Rav Yosef Chaim promised him ceremoniously.

Rav Yosef Chaim's words were like balm to Rabbi Naftali Hertz. Now he could proceed to the Brisker Rav's house, calm and collected.

As soon as the *seudah* was over, Rabbi Naftali Hertz hurried on to the home of his *rebbe*, the Brisker Rav. The Gaon of Brisk had not seen Rabbi Naftali—who numbered among his choice circle of disciples from the time he came to the Holy Land—for a long period. Now, as a sign of his high regard, deep respect and love for this *talmid*, the Brisker Rav turned to him with these words.

"Rabbi Naftali," he said, "I have a secret to reveal which I have never yet disclosed to the public. The Rashash's *siddur* is in my possession. You may look at it whenever you like. But since it was entrusted to my care by Rav Yaakov Leib, the *Rosh Av Beis Din*, I must ask you to look at it only in my home."

Rabbi Naftali's eyes lit up joyfully. Rav Yosef Chaim Sonnenfeld's words were coming true. But in reality, it was not so simple to go to the Brisker Rav's house just to examine the Rashash's *siddur*. Even greater and better men than he trembled when they stood before the Gaon of Brisk. A saintly man like Rabbi Naftali Hertz was reluctant to appear before his *rebbe* alone, merely to inspect a *siddur*.

The Rabbi of Jaffa thought about it and came up with a solution. There were two others among the Brisker Rav's *talmidim*, aside from Rav Yosef Chaim Sonnenfeld, who had been privileged upon occasion to enter the sanctuary and study from the revered *siddur*. These were Rabbi Shlomo Zalman Porush and Reb Leib Chafetz; Rabbi Naftali would join them.

And why did these particular *talmidim* deserve the honor denied others? That is a matter connected with an entirely different episode.

The Gaon of Brisk Strolls in the Chevron Hills

The Brisker *gaon* used to visit the Holy City of Chevron from time to time. Upon each visit he would be greeted by the two rabbis of the city, the Ashkenazi authority Rav Shimon Menashe and the Sefardic rabbi, Rav Eliyahu Mani.

He used to remain in Chevron for a week or two, inhaling the pure air of mountains that evoked nostalgic, ancient memories, purifying his mind for Torah study. In the evenings, he would go outside the city for a walk, the scholars of the city accompanying him and delighting in his conversation.

Reb Leib Chafetz and Rabbi Shlomo Porush also went to Chevron upon one of his visits and they, too, accompanied him on his twilight walks, one on his right and the other on his left.

On one particular day, Rav Yehoshua Leib was in high spirits and was most gracious to them. They drank his words thirstily, their own spirits elevated at this rare opportunity given to them to clarify certain questions and hear the *gaon's* good-natured replies. In passing, the Brisker Gaon evoked memories of the greatness of his father, Rav Binyamin Diskin, claiming that he had not begun to attain such heights.

"For example?" Reb Leib Chafetz ventured to ask.

"Let me tell you a story that happened when I was young," the *rav* replied. "When my father served as Rabbi of Vitebsk in Russia, a raging fire once broke out in the neighboring village. The flames penetrated the *beis knesses*, leaped into the *aron kodesh* and scorched the *Sefer Torah* inside. The villagers came to my father to ask him for a program of *teshuvah* to atone for the terrible tragedy.

"When I opened the door of our home and saw the burnt parchment of the scroll in the arms of one of the villagers, I fearfully asked the men what had happened. After hearing their story, I referred them to my father.

"As soon as my father saw the scorched scroll, he immediately fainted. It took much effort to revive him. Much later, when he regained consciousness, he was able to listen to their account and deal with the matter as he saw fit.

"That was enough to show me the difference between my father and myself."

The rabbis walked leisurely by the *rav's* side, a pleasant breeze caressing their faces, while stories and memories of the *rav* resounded like echoes from the past.

"When I came to Brisk to serve as rabbi, I heard that whenever a Jew was brought to the local court and had to swear, a policeman would be dispatched to the nearest synagogue to fetch a *Sefer Torah*. He would bring it to the court and the Jew would swear upon it.

"This practice had continued for years without anyone raising any protest. This Torah desecration disturbed me greatly and I forbade the congregation from practicing this shameful custom which bordered on *chilul Hashem*.

"Some days after my announcement, a Jew was called upon to testify in the local courts and the police officer was sent to the synagogue to fetch the *sefer* Torah. When he arrived, he was informed that the rabbi forbade removing the scroll for such purposes.

"The officer returned, reporting that the 'new rabbi' forbade bringing the scroll to be sworn upon. That very day I was summoned to the judge to explain my reasons for stopping the custom.

"I arrived at the appointed hour. The judge asked me if it was correct that I had forbidden removing the scroll.

"'Yes,' I replied.

"'Why?' he asked.

"'Because we dearly regard something that cost so much.'

"'How much did you pay for one Torah scroll?'

"'Tens of thousands of souls whose blood was spilled like water, who were tortured and burnt in its name, thousands who were tied to the stake to preserve one letter of what was written in it.'

"This explanation made a deep impression upon the gentile judge who immediately declared that henceforth the practice was to be abolished . . ."

In a whisper, the Brisker Rav added that from the time of his appearance in that court, the judge would frequently refer complicated cases to him for resolution.

As they were walking, the *rav* suddenly reminded himself of a letter he had received that week from Yerushalayim and turning to his companions, Reb Leib and Rabbi Shlomo Porush, he began speaking.

"I heard that a special assembly of Yerushalayim sages and scholars is scheduled to take place tonight," Rav Yehoshua Leib said, "to strengthen forces against the secular schools which representatives of the *Maskilim* abroad hope to establish in the

Holy City. Wouldn't you want to participate in this gathering, convened by Rav Yosef Chaim Sonnenfeld?"

Reb Leib Chafetz understood that his *rebbe* wished them to attend this meeting, and he immediately went to look for a wagon going to Yerushalayim.

At the moment that Rav Yosef Chaim opened the meeting with the verse, "Hashem, open my lips that my mouth may utter your praises," Reb Leib entered the auditorium.

Rabbi Shlomo Porush behaved otherwise. He did not hurry to leave his *rebbe*. In reply to the Brisker Rav's repeated question as to why he did not seem to be interested in attending the meeting in Yerushalayim, he replied as follows.

"First of all," he said, "I am preoccupied right now with the self-same *mitzvah* of revering the Torah and second, what can Rav Yosef Chaim innovate on this topic? His well-known refrain that 'it is an obligation to keep one's distance from the sinners' is quite familiar to me."

The Gaon of Brisk heard these words emitting from Rabbi Shlomo Porush's mouth and was aghast. His face turned white and even though he had regarded this *talmid* highly until now, he refused to speak to him any more. They returned to the *rav's* lodgings in silence and parted without exchanging a word.

The Brisker Rav returned to Yerushalayim a week later. Years passed and the incident was forgotten but in Rav Shlomo Porush's will to his son, he found it necessary to write the following words.

My beloved son, a father hands down to his son only the truth. That is why my advice to you is to consider the path which you choose.

1. Never refrain from attending gatherings of G-d-fearing

men for a matter concerning the strengthening of *Yiddishkeit*, for that is the will of our leaders, the *gedolei Yisrael*. I lost much by my indifference to one such gathering, and I never again was able to repair what I had wronged.

2. Become a follower of Rav Yosef Chaim Sonnenfeld, whose wisdom is as great as his righteousness. Follow his ways throughout your days and you will never falter. Personal experience once taught me that whoever separates from him, separates from life. See what lies ahead and you will benefit both in this world and in the next.

Your loving father,
Shlomo Porush

Recognition and Love for Those who Stand in the Breach

From the day that Reb Leib Chafetz walked with his *rebbe* in the Chevron hills, he gained the latter's admiration and a special measure of love was shown him.

Reb Leib did not suffice with mere participation in meetings but also bent his back against the smiters and turned cheek to the pluckers, in the struggle for pure, inviolate education.

The battle for pure education in the Holy City was a long and bloody one, countering the platform of the *Chovevei Zion* movement which threatened to destroy the *cheder* system, the venerable institution which promoted Torah and *yiras shamayim* in Yerushalayim. This group wanted to establish schools of secular studies bent upon shaking off the yoke of Torah responsibility and removing the jewel of modesty from the Jewish people.

Knowing that "from out of Zion shall come the Torah," the

Maskilim stormed in full force upon the pure *chinuch* in Yerushalayim.

In 5615, the walls of Yerushalayim shook with the arrival of Dr. Ludwig Frankel, missionary of the reformers, to found his Lemel school in Yerushalayim. Yerushalayim rabbis organized a united front against the impending danger, issuing an absolute ban on the school. The *Maskilim* were far from ready to give up, however.

There was a period of calm, then again they attempted to sink their claws into the city walls. The battle was renewed with increased force with the emigration of the Gaon of Brisk to Yerushalayim.

The Mazkeres Moshe Society of London decided to send financial support to Yerushalayim for the purpose of strengthening and improving the educational institutions of the *yishuv*, the old settlement and in the process, to introduce new subjects into the curriculum according to the demands of the times.

The Brisker Rav convened his *beis din*, renewed his original *cherem* against secular schools and turned to the Yerushalayim public to make them aware of the great danger upon the horizon.

And from then on, whenever the Brisker Rav saw that danger was threatening traditional education in Yerushalayim, he would send select *talmidim* to proclaim the ban in the synagogues.

The Gaon of Brisk taught a daily *shiur* to a group of young men of ability, sharp minds and a well-developed fear of Hashem. The first year his *shiurim* covered the tractate *Bava Basra*, but despite the fact that the daily *shiur* took four full hours and was taught on *erev Shabbos* as on *Shabbos*, on *erev Yom Tov* as on *Yom Tov* except for *Tishah b'Av*, in the summer of 5638 they only covered three pages, pondering over one phrase of *Tosfos* upon occasion for several consecutive days. Yet those who studied under him testify that he never repeated a *chiddush* twice!

In 5640, Dr. Herzberg, representative of the *Maskilim*, came to Yerushalayim to found an orphanage. For all appearances, his intentions were pure and wholesome but his true purpose was to wean the hearts of Jewish boys from underprivileged families away from Torah.

Dr. Herzberg wore a large velvet *kipah* on his head while the fringes of his *arba kanfos* garment fluttered above his clothing, an outward facade which served as a mask for his true nature. His hypocrisy was imitated by Chaim Hirshensohn from Yerushalayim who was appointed the administrator of the institution.

The Gaon of Brisk immediately smelled the impending danger inherent in the orphanage, however, and sent his two *talmidim*, Reb Leib Chafetz and Rabbi Shlomo Zalman Porush, to proclaim a ban which pertained to this institution as well. When the two messengers approached the place, a group of hoodlums attacked them and beat them, and it was only by a miracle that they escaped.

When the Gaon of Brisk heard what had happened to them, he went personally to visit them and wish them a speedy recovery.

Shortly later, Rabbi Shlomo Zalman was blessed with a son and despite the Brisker Rav's practice to shy away from honors and *kibbudim* as well as to refrain from eating outside his home, yet because he so valued Rabbi Shlomo Zalman's devotion and *mesiras nefesh* to preserve the purity of education, he veered from his usual custom and accepted the *sandakaus*. He participated in the *seudas mitzvah* which followed, to stress his affection for that *baal simchah.*

A short while after this episode, the Brisker Rav again sent Reb Leib Chafetz to proclaim the ban, this time on *Shabbos* when Yehudim Street was bathed in quiet. A group of hoodlums took advantage of the situation. They attacked and wounded him, then brought him to the Turkish authorities, claiming that he had been disturbing the peace. He was immediately imprisoned.

The arrest of Reb Leib Chafetz, one of the most important and respected men in the city, took the Yerushalayim public by storm and from all corners of the city, groups upon groups of men formed and converged upon his attackers. The city seethed.

On the following day, a large group of the Brisker Gaon's followers went forth, passing from street to street, blowing the *shofar* and proclaiming anew the ban against secular schools including the new orphanage of the *Maskilim.* In the presence of a large crowd, they proclaimed the *cherem* once again at the *Kosel* by Reb Zerach Braverman.

Rav Shmuel Salant, rabbi of the city, did not sit idly by either. Together with other leaders in the city, he issued a notice praising Reb Leib as a great scholar and a most pious person. Rav Shmuel also approached the authorities and by the morrow, Reb Leib was released.

When the people of Jaffa sought a suitable rabbi for their city, the Gaon of Brisk suggested Reb Leib Chafetz as the man for the position. Reb Leib went to Jaffa but returned to Yerushalayim shortly thereafter.

"I cannot be separated from my master and teacher, the Gaon of Brisk, for even a day," he said. Rabbi Naftali Hertz was appointed in his stead.

Such were some of the ways of Reb Leib Chafetz and Rabbi

Shlomo Zalman Porush, thanks to which they gained the respect and love of their *rebbe* to the extent that he was willing to entrust the Rashash's *siddur* in their hands for their perusal.

The Sun Sets at Midday

The year 5658 was a difficult one for the Jews of Yerushalayim and for world Jewry at large. In that year the Gaon of Brisk, Rav Yehoshua Leib Diskin, leader and commander of Jewry in his generation, passed away.

The crown was lifted, the diadem was removed and the general feeling was as if the sun had set at noon. The *rav's* health had been shaky for two weeks; his physicians attempted in vain to heal him but bit by bit as his weakness increased his strength dwindled until finally, on Tuesday, the twenty-fourth of *Teves*, the end came.

On that Tuesday, his condition was further complicated by severe pneumonia and his physicians hinted that his condition aroused grave danger, in fact, that his end was nigh.

When the *rav's* precarious state of health was publicized, an air of depression and tragedy settled all over the city. Men, women and children streamed to the synagogues; throngs ran to the *Kosel* and many went to *Kever Rachel* and to Chevron to pour out their hearts in prayer and supplication. Perhaps he would be pitied in Heaven and the faithful shepherd of the Jewish nation would not yet be claimed.

Angels and mortals fought over the holy ark.

Despite his extreme weakness, his soul scarcely had a body to contain it, his mental vigor did not leave him; his eyesight did not fade and his senses were as sharp as ever.

That great personality, Rav Yaakov Orenstein, one of his closer *talmidim*, used to relate this story.

"During the last week of his life, a Yerushalayim Jew entered with a question about a garment. The Gaon of Brisk refused to rule it permissible. Fearing that the *rav's* weakness had not allowed him to consider the matter with proper depth, the Jew returned on the following day with the identical question. But feeling embarrassed, he explained that it was a different garment. As soon as the *rav* looked at it, he said, 'Why did you return with the same question as yesterday?'

"The man became flustered and lied intentionally. 'No, *rebbe*! This is another garment.'

"'You must not lie,' said the *gaon*. 'I can tell you immediately how many threads were in the garment, so dare you say that?'

"The man broke down and wept, begging the *rav's* forgiveness for bothering him twice with the same question.

"The *talmidim* heard this and did not hesitate to seize the garment from the Jew's hands. They took it apart, thread by thread, and after several hours' work found to their amazement how exact their *rebbe* had been in his appraisal of the number of threads, not erring by even one, and all this with just one wink of his eyes, just days before his death!"

A similar incident occurred to a Yerushalayim Jew by the name of Yasha the druggist. He had received a letter from a relative in Hungary asking advice on some complicated matter. Reb Yasha did not dare accept the responsibility of deciding, and so he brought the letter, both sides of the paper covered with many words, to the Gaon of Brisk.

The *rav* glanced hastily at the letter and gave an answer on the spot. Reb Yasha left the house and began thinking, "The *rav* hardly read the letter! How could he have grasped the matter in just a few minutes?"

He retraced his steps, entered the *rav's* house once more and apologized in a trembling voice. "I just wanted to ask the *rav* if he read the entire letter," he said.

"And you surely did read the letter. Can you, then, repeat some of it?"

Reb Yasha was silent, astonished by the very question.

The *rav* set him at ease and with a smile on his lips said, "Rest assured, Reb Yasha, that I read the entire letter and here is proof. The letter contains one hundred and one words."

Reb Yasha could almost not find the door, so overcome was he with surprise. When he arrived home, he sat down and began counting the words on both sides of the letter and saw that the *rav* had grasped the exact number in a fleeting glance.

On *Motzei Shabbos, Erev Rosh Chodesh Shevat*, the angels bested the mortals and the great Gaon of Brisk was summoned to the *yeshivah shel maalah*.

The distress that swept the Holy City was deep and heavy. Its rabbi, Rav Shmuel Salant, convened his *beis din* and ruled that the funeral would be postponed to the following day despite the Yerushalayim custom not to keep the dead overnight. He feared that accidents might occur with the pressure and pushing of thousands in the narrow, darkened streets.

At the funeral, people discussed the long talk the Gaon of Brisk had delivered only three days before his death to his faithful confidante and *talmid*, Rav Yosef Chaim Sonnenfeld. The contents of this talk were to remain a sealed secret.

What did become public later was that the handwritten *siddur* of the Rashash which had been in the Brisker Rav's possession, was transferred to Rav Yosef Chaim. It was to be transmitted in turn, to the greatest *mekubal* of the Beis El *yeshivah*, the Rashash's own *yeshivah*.

The Last Journey of the Holy *Siddur*

When Rav Yosef Chaim set about fulfilling his *rebbe's* last request to give the *siddur* to the greatest *mekubal* of the Beis El *yeshivah*, he was struck by the thought that there was no person more suitable than the Sefardic Rabbi of Chevron, the great Rav Eliyahu Mani.

When Rav Eliyahu Mani had come to Eretz Yisrael, he had gone to the Beis El *yeshivah* to study. When he was about thirty, despite his youth, he had studied in partnership with the man then at the *yeshivah's* helm, Rav Rafael Yedidya Abulafya.

Having fasted for many years, his body had become weakened and he had gone to live in Chevron where the pure air was beneficial to his health. He was crowned as rabbi and founded the *beis midrash* and *yeshivah* Beis Yaakov, which he himself headed, along the guidelines of the Yerushalayim Beis El *yeshivah*.

The decision to transmit the *siddur* to Rav Eliyahu was actually not Rav Yosef Chaim's own. He had learned of the Brisker Rav's esteem of this *mekubal* several years before, this only because of the latter's firm stand for the Brisker Rav's own lifetime labor in Yerushalayim—the preservation of pure education.

Rav Eliyahu was one of the few Sefardic figures, like a lone tree upon a plain, who stood steadfastly, unbending, against the storm of *haskalah* which had begun flooding traditional education. This was why Rav Yosef Chaim concluded that Rav

Eliyahu Mani was the man whom his *rebbe* had referred to.

When Rav Eliyahu had come to live in Chevron, he had noted the wasteland; there was neither Torah or piety. He had dedicated all of his energy to fanning anew the flame of Torah in this Holy City. For those of ability and talent for study, he had established tents of Torah which they could dwell in, and for people tied up with business pursuits or crafts, he had established regular study periods. Slowly, the spirit of Torah had spread throughout the ancient City of the Patriarchs.

Rav Eliyahu Mani's success in fanning the flame of Torah and *yiras shamayim* in the city which had already been penetrated by the rays of "enlightenment," had won him to be sure, no few adversaries who schemed to sabotage his work.

One time a wealthy man named Tshilibi, came from Istanbul to settle in Chevron. His sons, who remained in Turkey, were very wealthy as well. This Tshilibi bought a large plot of land outside the Jewish quarter upon which he intended to build a magnificent palace. In course of construction, a quarrel erupted between the owner and one of the laborers. The latter demanded a large sum for reparations and took the case to court.

Tshilibi was summoned to the *beis din* to reply against the charges, but he was highly insulted. He, the wealthy and prestigious personality was being asked to defend himself against the claim of a petty, common laborer! Before an old fashioned court, no less? Tshilibi ignored the summons.

He was called a second time and again refused to appear. On the third time, a warning accompanied the summons, cautioning him that if he refused to stand for a *din Torah* the *beis din* would issue a "*ksav seiruv*," a writ of refusal, after which he would no longer be allowed to remain in Chevron.

This finally convinced him to appear before the *beis din*. He was found guilty and was forced to pay the full sum demanded by the plaintiff. Tshilibi seethed with anger and joined the forces of Rav Eliyahu Mani's opponents. He poured his money and wrath into undermining the foundations of pure education which Rav Eliyahu had struggled to establish with such self-sacrifice.

Fully appraising Rav Eliyahu's virtue, the rabbis of Yerushalayim issued a proclamation supporting his mighty accomplishments, warning his opponents to heed his fire, noting that the Almighty would certainly avenge this *tzaddik's* honor.

That warning issued by the Yerushalayim rabbis was carried out in full.

One of Tshilibi's sons who lived in Istanbul and supported his father's battle against the *Talmud Torah* in Chevron by sending funds, suddenly became critically ill. The father was summoned to his son's bedside. When he recovered and Tshilibi left the city to return to Chevron, the son again became sick and again the father was called to his side.

This was repeated a third time, but Tshilibi's eyes were blinded as were his ears, and they stopped absorbing the Heavenly warning. When he had reached Damascus, he was called back to his son's bedside for the third time, but when he arrived in Istanbul it was already too late.

The death struck Rav Eliyahu Mani's opponents like a bolt of lightening. This was unmistakable evidence of the rabbi's sanctity and might, showing clearly that whoever threatened to touch him was immediately scalded. These men now began pressing upon Tshilibi to retract and yield. In *Tammuz* of 5646, a peace settlement was signed between the two camps. Tshilibi's followers accepted all the *rav's* instructions concerning matters of education in the city and peace was again restored.

It was this unequivocal and fearless stand of Rav Eliyahu in a struggle for untampered education—which to the Brisker Rav was the crux of Jewry's challenge in these latter generations— that won for the former an extra measure of respect.

And this is what Rav Yosef Chaim understood his *rebbe* to have intended when he told him to transmit the sacred *siddur* which he possessed.

Rav Eliyahu Mani received the *siddur* from Rav Yosef Chaim and when he heard the Brisker Gaon's last words, he became filled with a great joy. From that day on, for a year and a half, he delved into the Rashash's Torah day and night.

Every *Erev Yom Kippur*, Rav Eliyahu Mani would bless his many descendants and offer them guidelines for the coming year, directing each one to the path he was to follow. He would put particular emphasis upon *tzeddakah* and on that occasion, each individual would receive a coin from him to distribute to the poor.

On the *Erev Yom Kippur* of the 5659, a significant change was evident in Rav Eliyahu's words. This time, he spoke at length about the necessary preparations for the journey which every Jew must eventually make.

On the day after *Yom Kippur* he called the head of the *Chevra Kadisha* and gave him instructions for after his death. From then on his daily schedule doubled. Everything that he had been accustomed to accomplish from one *Yom Kippur* to another, he now condensed in the time until *Pesach* as if he must make haste for the journey.

In the beginning of the month of *Tammuz* that year, he summoned his eldest son to him. "I was born in *Tammuz* and I will return my soul to my Creator in *Tammuz*," he said. "Please, guard the purity of *chinuch* which is the foundation of the sanctity of the Jewish people, here in our city, for I have sacrificed myself for it these many years."

On Friday, the eighth of *Tammuz* 5659, the *rav* returned his soul to Hashem.

The Rashash's *Siddur* Is Published

Before he died, Rav Eliyahu Mani wrote an urgent letter to Rav Yosef Chaim Sonnenfeld, informing him in brief of a wonderful dream he had just had that night.

"My *rebbe*, Rav Rafael Yedidya Abulafya, stood before me, another man by his side. Rav Rafael Yedidya pointed to this old man and said, 'I have come to you with my master, the Rashash, to inform you that the time has come to publish the *siddur* and release it to the world. Do it quickly . . .'"

The handwritten manuscript was brought immediately to Yerushalayim where Rav Yosef Chaim Sonnenfeld's son, Rabbi Yaakov Meir, personally supervised the printing. He was assisted in this *mitzvah* by the precious Yerushalayim Jews, Rabbi Reuven Haz and Rabbi Shmuel Kirshenbaum, after preparation of the manuscript by the *mekubal* Reb Yom Tov Yedid Halevi and his son Rabbi Eliezer.

The *siddur* was brought to print after eleven years together with the annotations of Rav Chaim Shaul Dvik. It was known as *Chessed Ve'emes*.

The five men who, on the fifteenth of *Marcheshvan*, 5671, had appeared before Rav Chaim Berlin, were the very men who had attended to the printing of this sacred *siddur* and who now, just before its release, had requested his *haskamah* (approval) signifying that the finished product corresponded exactly with the handwritten original.

It was for this privilege, of granting his approval to this momentous undertaking, that Rav Chaim Berlin had donned his *Shabbos* clothing and with feelings of exalted *simchah*, had affixed his name to the paper.